LEBANESE
COOKING
AN INTRODUCTION TO THIS SPECIAL
MIDDLE EASTERN CUISINE

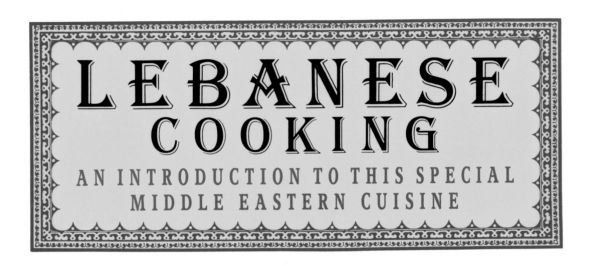

LEBANESE
COOKING
AN INTRODUCTION TO THIS SPECIAL
MIDDLE EASTERN CUISINE

SUSAN WARD

CHARTWELL
BOOKS, INC.

A QUINTET BOOK

Published by Chartwell Books
A Division of Book Sales, Inc.
110 Enterprise Avenue
Secaucus, New Jersey 07094

This edition produced for sale
in the U.S.A., its territories
and dependencies only

ISBN 1–55521–779–6

This book was designed and produced by
Quintet Publishing Limited
6 Blundell Street
London N7 9BH

Creative Director: Richard Dewing
Designer: Chris Dymond
Project Editor: William Hemsley
Food Photographer: Trevor Wood
Photographs of Lebanon: Alistair Duncan/
Middle East Archive

Typeset in Great Britain by
Central Southern Typesetters, Eastbourne
Manufactured in Hong Kong by
Regent Publishing Services Limited
Printed in Hong Kong by
Leefung-Asco Printers Limited

CONTENTS

INTRODUCTION
A COUNTRY AND A CUISINE

My Lebanon . . . was a cloak of many colors. Beirut was Levantine to the heart, astute, multilingual, many-minded and with an element of sheer bawdy wickedness. Tripoli up north . . . was Sunni, fanatic, austere. Tyre and Sidon slept in the sand by the sea. The people of the plain were not the people of the mountain, a mile away .

Thus wrote Albion Ross, American journalist and *aficionado* of Lebanon, in 1957, when the troubles that would eventually overtake it were first erupting. Both recurrent civil war and the escalation of the Arab-Israeli conflict have devastated what was once the pride of the eastern Mediterranean – a democracy on a nation of minorities, all living in a golden-green land half the size of Wales. Of course, that "cloak of many colors" was sewn with faulty thread. The seams came undone, and the fabled tolerance of the artificial nation carved from Syria by the French Mandate of 1860–6, and made independent in 1946, was shown to be based on a myth the populace itself could no longer afford to believe.

The sun rises over fishing boats in the harbor at Tyre.

A farmer in the Bekkah Valley using traditional methods.

refugees. The two groups have traditionally been almost as suspicious of one another as of non-believers. The very slightly smaller Christian population is dominated by the Maronites, an ancient sect, united to Rome since the thirteenth century. The Maronites, by virtue of their commercial success and historical ties with France, have long been the most educated, cosmopolitan group in the country, and have actively cultivated the sophistication associated with all things French. It is largely a result of their powerful influence that the French tongue is almost as widely heard as Arabic, the official language; a triumph of their business acumen that Beirut became the "Paris of the Middle East". To the honeypot of Beirut came foreign adventurers, investors, tourists and twentieth-century settlers from Europe; it is an indication of the city's pre-civil war international bias that masses at Beirut's two major Roman Catholic churches were held not only in French and Arabic, but also in English, Italian, German, Spanish and, occasionally, Polish.

The other important minorities include the Druse, a secretive religious sect whose feats of arms are legendary; Orthodox and Catholic Greeks; Armenians and Syrians; and a small community of Jews.

It is the Arabic-Muslim tradition that has ensured the survival of herbed or spiced olive oil and lemon juice as the ubiquitous dressing and marinade; that has confirmed the domination of yogurt over cream (a French contribution); that accounts for the prevalence of lamb-based meat dishes and the absence of pork; that has developed the range of *meze* to triumphant heights, and has incorporated a variety of nuts into savory dishes and made them one of the mainstay of sweets, pastries and such rare delicacies as green almond jelly.

It is the French-Maronite influence that has brought wine to the table and vinegar into the kitchen; that has introduced new and succulent vegetables into cultivation and the Syrian truffle into fine Beirut restaurants; that has refined the sometimes agressive spicing of the East into a subtlety appreciated by Westerners. These two main traditions have historically welcomed the contributions of neighbors and the other ethnic communities: the dates of the Iraqis and the dried fruit dishes of the Jews and Palestinians; the beef dishes and meat stews of the Armenians; the pomegranate seeds and sumac of the Iranians and Syrians; the pasta of the Italians.

This brief introduction to the tragedy that has overtaken one of the most beautiful, productive and culturally fascinating parts of the Middle East may seem out of place in a cook book. However, to ignore the divisions that have brought it about is also to misunderstand the diversity and richness of Lebanon's heritage, reflected in the diversity and richness of its table. Lebanon has played host to invaders, refugees, settlers and merchants since 2000 BC; today it claims to be the only country in the world whose population is composed entirely of minorities, though all call themselves Arabs. These divisions, drawn along religious lines, are reflected in the influences that have united to create Lebanese cuisine.

The large Muslim population is divided almost equally between Sunnis and Shiites, the latter group augmented in the past 20 years by many Palestinian

Before the war, Lebanon was the richest agricultural region in the Eastern Mediterranean after Israel. Topographically, it is a kind of mini-California. A warm coastal plain, cultivated with citrus fruit and bananas, gives way to foothills covered in vineyards and orchards of apricots, plums and peaches; soil-poor outcrops provide adequate subsistence for olive and fig trees, goats and sheep. The rains falling on the high mountains behind feed the agrarian paradise of the Bekkah Valley, nestled between the first mountain range and the second, larger barrier straddling the eastern border with Syria.

The River Litani, its tributaries and canals, are responsible for the richness of the Bekkah, truly a "land of milk and honey". Here grow the plumpest fruits and vegetables, and here graze the fattest livestock; the vines looking down on the valley grow on the rootstock brought by the Jesuits almost 200 years ago.

Along the rocky banks of the Bardoni, an offshoot of the Litani, lies the resort of Zahle. In better times, tourists and the inhabitants of Beirut and the coast would flock to its rustic cafés and outdoor restaurants on the weekends, to eat *mezze*, drink coffee, wine and *arak*, and smoke the traditional *narghileh*, or water pipe. Today, the tables are largely empty – former patrons now more concerned with survival than good living. In Beirut itself, the hotels are vacant; the swimming pools, dry holes. The curtain has rung down on the famous Casino du Liban, 16 miles up the coast – on its floorshows, gambling, restaurant complex and theater. Only the people whose lives are tied to the country remain.

But optimism is the lifeblood of the Lebanese people, and there are signs that it is flowing with renewed energy. A solution to the Arab-Israeli conflict would mean another chance for a viable Lebanese state, whatever compromises might have to be made between interest groups. Already Lebanese government tourist offices are back in operation, though as yet they have little to promote in their home country. That, we hope, is to come; meanwhile the delights and seductions of Lebanese cooking are becoming more widely known through restaurants, delicatessens and even supermarkets in the West. If we can share in the gustatory pleasures of the country now, how much more eager will we be to sample them in the sunny Mediterranean land from which they come?

LEBANESE EATING – IN AND OUT

Farmers and shepherds are hard at work soon after sunrise; shops and offices are usually open by 8.30 am. This is the lightest meal of the day, consisting typically of *labneh* (yogurt cheese) with *khoubz* (Arab bread). Olives, dates, fresh fruits, honey and nuts will also share the table. Country people may eat a bowl of *ful medames* (small brown fava beans), while eggs, fried or hard-boiled, are another alternative.

Lunch, taken between 1 pm and 3 pm, can be the main meal among rural folk, but more usually it is an abbreviated spread of *meze* with fresh *khoubz*. In Beirut and other large towns, snack bars have proliferated, as they have in Western cities; they are life-savers for the office worker.

Dinner, for most Lebanese, is the main meal of the day, taken with the whole family. Eaten between 8 pm and 11pm, it consists of a selection of *meze* – the number and quality of which are dictated by the occasion and the prosperity of the family – grilled meat or poultry (or, on the coast, fish), accompanied by burghul – the usual grain – or less frequently, by rice.

Among Beirut's middle classes, and throughout Lebanon's large Christian communities, the segregation common in the rest of the Arab world between men and women at meals is not customary. Lebanese women are seen eating (and drinking) in restaurants, and they entertain mixed company in their homes.

In Beirut before the troubles, every type of international restaurant drew Lebanese citizens and tourists. Today, the restaurant scene has disintegrated, but the expertise and experience are there to be resurrected when better times return.

Of the Lebanese Arab-style restaurants (*mat'am*) and cafés, some specialize. There are restaurants serving barbecued lamb dishes (*mat'am lahem mashwi*) and fish and seafood (*mat'am samak*); there are non-alcoholic snack bars serving *shawarma* (*mah'em asir*), patisseries (*helaewayat shami*) and cafés offering *mezze* and *arak* (*kas arak wi mezze*).

Snow melts in the mountains above a village and terraced fields.

TREASURES OF THE LEBANESE DELICATESSEN

Most Middle-Eastern delicatessens in Britain and the United States have a preponderance of either Lebanese-produced or Lebanese-style staples and prepared foods on their shelves. This is partly because of the traditional role of the Lebanese as businessmen/importers, and partly because of the especially high regard in which the Lebanese refinements of the Arab table are held. The varied influences that have shaped the country have also given the food a cosmopolitan appeal, in both preparation and presentation. Although many of the same dishes are found in neighboring Syria and Jordan – and even, with a slightly different accent, in Egypt or Turkey – much of what we Westerners today appreciate as "Middle-Eastern" cuisine has, somewhere along the way, been edited and elevated by Lebanese taste and polish.

Imagine that you have entered a typical Middle-Eastern food shop. On narrow wire racks you may find a range of dried spices and herbs, some prepacked by large firms, others in hand-labeled plastic bags produced by members of a small family business. On rows of shelves are displayed a selection of largely unfamiliar dried or canned pulses and grains – beans in shades of brown, white and red; green, brown or red lentils; and packets and boxes of burghul, semolina (North African couscous and Levantine *moghrabieh*), and Egyptian and Syrian *fariek* (whole wheat). Farther along are bottles of olive oil, rose and orange flower waters, and syrups, in slight variations by a myriad of producers, for cooks are noted for devotion to their favorite brands.

There will be more shelves – or perhaps a central island – piled with fresh fruits, vegetables and selected herbs. Many of the vegetables are ones less frequently encountered in this country, such as fresh shelled broad beans (*ful akdar*); okra (*bamia*); small, pale green, pear-shaped zucchini (*kousa*), baby purple or striped egg plant (*bazinjan*) and fresh green olives for home pickling. In trays, or packaged in bags will be dried fruits – figs (*tihn*), dates (*tamar* or *bayleh*), apricots

(*mishmish*) – as well as nuts and dried seeds (*mohamahsat*). The Arab love of nuts has been developed to an obsession in Lebanon; in addition to the usual plain unsalted varieties for cooking – in Lebanon mainly pistachios (*fosto*), pine nuts (*sonoba*), almonds (*lohz*), cashews and, to a lesser extent, walnuts (*en'gamael*) – there will always be a selection specially prepared for nibbling: lemon-flavored or salted pistachios, or pistachios encased whole in a kind of sweet brittle cake (*fosto illieh*); two or three kinds of salted almonds (*lohz*); cashews and peanuts (*ful sudani*). The melon seeds on offer make a popular snack; while sesame seeds (*sum sum*) – either plain or toasted – appear in everything from *tahini* to breads and desserts.

Dominating the delicatessen will probably be two or three cold cabinets. Those hidden at the back of the shop contain regional cheeses and homemade yogurt, prepared spiced ground meat for kebabs, and a selection of *mezze* and salads: *sambousek* and *fatayeer* (savory pastries stuffed with meat, spinach or cheese); deep-fried *kibbeh bi shamiyeh* (ground lamb and burghul cases stuffed with a lamb and pine nut mixture), *houmus* and *tabbouleh* (cracked wheat salad). Ranged along the counter are jars of oil-pickled cheeses (*shanklish*); below, great earthenware bowls hold black or green olives, some awash in marinades ripe with whole chilies and lemon slices, others in pools as black as pitch.

In the glass case facing the street will be the jewels of the collection, a mouth-watering display of small sweet pastries, most with a dusting of bright green, ground pistachio. They draw the eyes of passers-by, tempting them into this gastronomic Aladdin's cave. The selection may include varieties of *mam'oul*, sweet-dough balls and ovals filled with chopped dates, pistachios or walnuts; crisp phyllo-covered pastries like *asabieh* – cigar-shaped "fingers" filled with chopped cashews – or *bohaj*, "packets" enfolding pistachio or mixed nuts. Pride of place is ceded to the internationally renowned *baklava* – diamond-shaped slices sticky

A vegetable barrow in a Beirut market.

with perfumed syrup, whose typical Lebanese filling is pistachio or cashew (rather than the walnuts common in Turkey and Greece).

To lovers of Middle-Eastern food – whether by birthright or conversion – crossing the threshold of a store such as this is never simply "shopping". Like the French, the Levantine peoples take great interest in their food; they live to eat, rather than eat to live. Deciding upon purchases necessitates discussion of quality and debate upon methods and recipes – spiced with gossip or an exchange of family news. As in the

"old country", food shops act as centers for the community – perhaps even more so in a Western metropolis, where links with tradition are harder for people to maintain.

As for the Western initiate, the elements of epicureanism, fascination and curiosity are inextricably combined. There is always something new to appreciate – a packet never noticed before, a different-shaped pastry to try, a taste to experience. It takes a spirit of adventure of course – to ask, to buy and, ultimately, to try – but the rewards far exceed the effort.

A-Z OF INGREDIENTS AND SPECIALITIES

The following ingredients and staples are those that are typically Middle-Eastern, with particular emphasis on items characteristic of Lebanon. They will be found in most good delicatessens and/or Middle-Eastern shops. I have used the Arabic name (in approximate phonetic English) as the identifying term when it is the one by which a dish or ingredient is commonly known, even among Westerners.

Arak: a spirit distilled from grape juice and flavored with aniseed. Similar to Greek *ouzo,* it is somewhat lighter in flavor and less syrupy in consistency.

Basturma: a cured and smoked fillet of beef, dark red in the center and covered with a thick coating of spice. It is a variation of Israeli *pastourma* and a predecessor of the better-known Armenian *pastrami.*

Beans: the most popular include light-brown broad beans (*ful nabed*) and the small, darker brown *ful medames,* with their characteristic black "eye". The latter are a much beloved staple of everyday life, eaten as a snack, at breakfast and in main dishes. Other common varieties include white haricot beans (*ful baladi sa'ideh*) and fresh green beans (*loubieh*), which are served as a *mezze*/salad, accompaniment or stewed with meat. (See also *houmus,* below)

Burghul: wheat grain that has been lightly cooked, dried and ground, either to a fine or medium-coarse grade. It is available unhusked (wholewheat) or, more commonly, husked (bleached). Fine-ground burghul is used for making *kibbeh* and *tabbouleh*; the medium-coarse for stuffings and stews such as *imjadra.*

Bread: the undifferentiated Arabic term *koubhz* – "bread" – is used for very different types of this staple, from the common flat individual round, to wholewheat sheets, to the sesame-covered versions. In rural areas it is baked by the family in earthen ovens; in towns and villages it is the province of the baker. Bread is eaten in great quantities throughout all meals.

Cheeses: Lebanese cheeses are usually very white, made from the milk of goats or sheep. The most common is *labneh,* homemade or available prepared, which is a condensed yogurt used both as a dip and in cooking. *Shanklish* are little balls of *labneh,* coated in mint, thyme or other herbs, and bottled or served covered in oil. *Anari,* a sheep's milk cheese, is available both wet – as a kind of ricotta – and dry for grating. *Gibeh beideh* is a salty white cheese similar to Greek Feta, which is usually substituted for it abroad. *Kallaje,* and the more familiar Turkish *halloumi,* are sharper, maturer cheeses with a rather rubbery texture, often served fried with bread or eggs. Syrian *gibneh jaduleh* ("braided cheese") has the appearance its name implies. It has much the same consistency as mozzarella and is used in the same way.

Green beans in olive oil.

Lebanese bread.

Coffee and **Tea:** *gowhwa* (coffee) and *shay* (tea) are both consumed in great quantities, though coffee is undoubtedly the king of Lebanese drinks, with its "prime time" after dinner. Both beverages are served in small, handleless cups – tea often in glasses. Unlike Turkish coffee, the Lebanese version is decanted into a pot before serving, so it does not possess the heavy sediment associated with much Middle-Eastern-styled coffee. The coffee and sugar are brewed together, so that the diner must let his host or waiter know whether he wishes his coffee very sweet (*sokah ziyaday*), medium (*mazbout*) or without sugar (*sayeday*). Lebanese coffee is traditionally flavored with ground cardamom (which can be added to the freshly ground coffee when you buy it from a shop). (Less frequently, cinnamon – which is supposed to be an aphrodisiac – is substituted for the cardamom.) After several cups of coffee following the meal, Lebanese diners then move on to several cups of tea.

Both tea and coffee are also enjoyed anytime during the day, and cafés are full of men (though in Lebanon women, too, frequent restaurants and cafés) smoking the water pipe (*nargileh*) and passing the time of day. Tea is served sweet, but less so than the North African version, and the mint leaves typically added to Arab tea are not left to stew. Rather they are added to the pot – or the glass itself – just before the tea is served.

Flower waters: orange flower water and rosewater are used in desserts and sweets, notably in *mam'oul* and phyllo-wrapped pastries. Orange flower water is also boiled with water to produce Lebanese "white coffee", a digestive appreciated after meals.

Houmus: the term is used both for the whole chickpeas and for the creamy paste made from the ground pulses and seasoned with lemon juice, olive oil, garlic, herbs and spices (page 36). It is served as a *mezze,* but also accompanies broiled dishes such as chicken, shish kebab or *shawarma* (q.v.).

Kishik: a dehydrated wheat and yogurt product, used more in Iranian cooking, but which has certain limited uses in the Lebanese kitchen. Available in packets and in bottles, it must be reconstituted with water before being used in dips and to make *Manakeish bi Za'atar* (pizza-like dough topped with *kishik*, thyme and olive oil, a variation of *Lahem bi Ajine*, page 44).

Malbalm: long, brownish-pink sticks with a waxen appearance made from grape juice boiled down to a gum-like consistency and mixed with nuts. It is a sweetmeat sold on the streets and in shops from Turkey to Egypt, though that available in Western delicatessens usually comes from Cyprus.

Moghrabieh: tiny semolina balls sold dried in packets, used to thicken Lebanese chicken soup. It is not an ingredient you will encounter in restaurants or at Lebanese-style dinner parties – it is a peasant dish, like the rustic soups thickened with tapioca pearls in parts of Western Europe.

Nuts: the most popular Lebanese nuts are pistachios (*fosto*) and pine nuts (*sonoba*); both are used across the range of cooking, from *mezze* to sweetmeats and desserts. To a lesser degree, almonds (*lohz*), cashews (*kaju*) and walnuts (*en'gamael*) make an appearance.

Houmus garnished with paprika and parsley.

Sweet spiced pistachios.

Oils: the other major cooking agent used by Lebanese cooks, in addition to *samneh* (q.v.), is olive oil. Since olives themselves are treated with such imagination and pickled in so many ways, it is not surprising that olive oil holds a valued place in the kitchen. Less flavorsome oils – vegetable and sunflower – have made few inroads into Lebanese cooking. A traditional cooking fat, *alyeh*, obtained from exceptionally fattened sheep (particularly from the tail) was once popular in the mountain and desert regions of the Levant, but is much less used today.

Phyllo: a pastry made from flour, water and oil originally developed in ancient Greece. It is rolled extremely fine to an almost paper-thin consistency, and is used for both sweet and savory pastries, including *sambousek* and *baklava*. Difficult to make at home, except for a cook experienced in its preparation, phyllo is available in commercial packets composed of large sheets.

Pomegranate seeds: although the seeds are used primarily in Iranian and Syrian cooking, they make their appearance in some Lebanese stuffings and salads, providing a piquant, slightly sour-sweet taste.

Samneh: this is simply clarified butter. In Lebanon it has a distinctive flavor, since it is usually made from sheep's (or less commonly, goat's) milk. When made from cow's milk, it is the same as Indian *gee*, which still has a stronger taste than ordinary butter. It was developed before the days of refrigeration, and its long cooking and subsequent refinement from impurities means that it will keep for several months and can withstand higher temperatures than ordinary butter. However, in most cases where a traditional recipe calls for *samneh*, ordinary butter or a mixture of butter and oil will be adequate, though lacking *samneh*'s pungent undertones.

Sausages: Levantine sausages are usually made from lamb or beef, and are made to be broiled over a fire. They include *makaneh*, and the very spicy dried *sujuk*, sometimes cut into pieces and mixed with *batatas harras* (Fried Potatoes, page 101) or other vegetable dishes which a cook wants to "lift".

Shawarma: a large conical hunk of sliced raw lamb and fat, compressed around a vertical split. This stands before a special gas or electric fire, which broils the meat as it rotates, basting itself. The thin slices cut off as the outer layers of the meat cooks are stuffed into Arab bread pockets, together with onions and a spicy sauce. Special equipment is needed both to make the compressed *shawarma* and to cook it, so it is served in special snack bars or street stalls. It is a close relative of Turkish döner kebab.

Tahini: a paste made from ground toasted sesame seeds emulsified with olive oil, lemon juice and garlic. This basic staple of Lebanese and Arabic cuisine can be made at home, but is often bought prepared in bottles (preferable to the canned variety). It is used to make dips and other dishes, but can also be used on its own as a dip.

Vine leaves: in Lebanon vines grow abundantly around doorways and over verandahs, so that fresh young leaves are always available. Abroad, they must often be bought in plastic packets or canned, and preserved in brine. They must be soaked and drained before they are used.

Wine and **Beer:** the Bekkah Valley is the center of Lebanese wine growing; the first vines were planted by Jesuit missionaries in 1857. They are still in production, despite the war. The best vineyards are Château Musar, a heavy dark red, and the rosés, Château Kefraya and Domaine des Tourelles.

The best-known Lebanese brands of beer are Almaza and Laziza.

Yogurt: in Lebanon, yogurt is usually made from sheep's or goat's whole milk, and is a much richer, thicker product than we are used to in the West. It is used in salads, main courses and desserts; drained and condensed it becomes *labneh*, which is a form of creamy sour cheese.

Cucumber and yogurt salad (page 59).

THE LEBANESE HERB GARDEN

*Denotes the herbs most frequently used.

Coriander

*Coriander (*kuzbarak*): although it looks very much like flat-leaved parsley, this herb has a more acrid taste which makes it suitable for all types of savory cooked dishes, salads and *mezze*.

Dill (*shabeth*): a dry-climate, feathery member of the umbellifer family, which is good when used as a flavoring for fish and salads.

Marjoram

Wild Marjoram (*rigani*): the wild variety is preferred to the cultivated in Lebanon; it imparts a distinctive peppery flavor to marinades for kebabs and to a few casseroles. Wild marjoram does not grow in Britain or the United States.

*Mint (*na'na*): spearmint and peppermint grow abundantly throughout the Middle East and are the two varieties of the large mint family used in cooking. Mint is added fresh to tea, salads and meat dishes, marrying particularly well with cucumber and lamb. Donkeys bearing great panniers overflowing with mint cuttings clip-clop down highways from Morocco to Turkey.

Mustard and Cress (*barbe'en*): a sharp-flavored salad ingredient and garnish, recognizable from its tiny double leaves topping each stem.

*Parsley (*bagdunish*): parsley used in the Middle East is always flat-leaved with, some maintain, a slightly stronger flavor than the curly variety.

Sage

Sage (*maraniyeh*): used in marinades for kebabs, roasted meats and stuffings. It has a dominating taste which should be treated with care.

Thyme

Thyme (*za'atar*): makes an appearance in stuffings and stews, though not with the frequency it does in the western Mediterranean.

THE LEBANESE SPICE CABINET

Denotes the spices most frequently used.

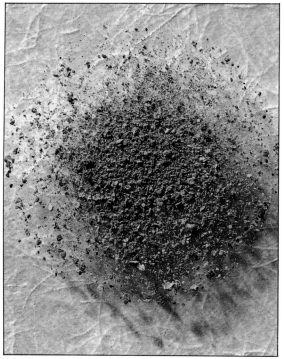

Allspice

Black pepper (*filfil aswad*): used as much in Arabic as in Western cooking.

Caraway (*karawayeh*): the seeds of this relative of aniseed and fennel are used in salads and savories; occasionally in Arab pastries.

Caraway

***Allspice** (*bahar hahilu*): perhaps the premier spice in Lebanese cookery. The small round berries of the Jamaican pepper tree seem to encapsulate the flavors of cloves, cinnamon and nutmeg, though allspice has no relation to any of them. Since these three spices are much appreciated in Lebanon, allspice is often used in dishes where they might otherwise appear, or in combination with them for added impact.

Aniseed (*yansoun*): the flavoring used in making *arak* (see the A-Z earlier), aniseed is also used in savory dishes and sweets.

Black cherry kernel (*mahlab*): this uniquely Arabic spice is made from the pale brown kernel found inside the pit of the black cherry. Sold whole, it must be ground to a powder. Although it is used mainly in Syrian and Iranian cooking, it appears occasionally in Lebanese pastries and breads.

***Cardamom** (*hab'han*): fresh green cardamom pods are used in savory dishes, though less than in India. The black seeds are ground to flavor coffee (q.v.).

***Cinnamon** (*kirfy*): cinnamon, the inner bark of trees found in Sri Lanka, shaved into quills, was an important trade commodity to the Levant long before the Crusades. It appears in a large number of Lebanese dishes, flavoring the spectrum of dishes from *mezze* to pastries and desserts.

Chili (*bisbas*): fresh thin green chilies are found in the basket of vegetables presented at the beginning of a Lebanese meal; beware, they are fiery! Green chilies and dry red chilies also appear in several savory dishes, though not as frequently as they do in North African cuisine.

Nutmeg (*jawajz a'tib*): the ground or grated nut appears in sweet or savory dishes, although allspice (q.v.) is more commonly used.

Paprika (*filfil hilu*): this spice is not widely exploited in Lebanon. It is used mostly as a garnish.

Saffron (*za'faran*): sparingly used in Lebanese cooking, primarily as a coloring for rice. It does not receive the respect it gets in Iranian and Indian cooking.

Sumac (*sumac*): this is a spice made from the crushed berries of the sumac tree. It is used primarily in Iranian cooking, but appears in Lebanese *Fatayeer* (page 41) and is occasionally used as a condiment like pepper, to be sprinkled over salads and savory dishes. It is an acquired taste, having a bitter flavor.

Turmeric (*kurkum*): like saffron, this is used infrequently and sparingly as a colorant for rice dishes. Its flavor is bitter and its color more garish than that of saffron.

Turmeric.

Cloves

Cloves (*kabsh kurnful*): like cinnamon, these hardened flower buds have long been an important part of Lebanese cuisine, both sweet and savory.

Cumin (*kammun*): less popular than in North Africa, cumin nevertheless is grown locally and used in salads, meat dishes and marinades.

Lebanese spice mix: this does not have a standard name in Arabic, nor is there a standard recipe; it is devised by each cook to taste. It is made ahead of time, in order for the flavors to mingle, and used when required. A guideline proportion might be 4 parts ground cinnamon, 1 part ground cloves, 1 part ground chili, 1 part green cardamom pods.

SUGGESTED MENUS

A SUMMER LUNCH PARTY

Chilled Artichoke Soup

◆

Sardine-stuffed Lemons (*Hamid Mashi wi Saerdin*)
Stuffed Vine Leaves (*Warah Inab*)

◆

Beef and Barley Salad
Ful Medames

◆

Orange Yogurt Cake

A HOT AND COLD VEGETARIAN PARTY

Cheese Balls (*Shanklish*)
Lebanese Avocado Dip (*Avocado bi Tahini*)
with Arab Bread (*Khoubz*) or Pita
Beirut Olives

◆

Chick-pea Balls (*Falafel*)
Savory *Baklava*
Lebanese Bread Salad (*Fattoush*)

◆

Vegetable Layer (*Mousakha'a*)
Lentils and Burghul (*Imjadra*)

◆

Orange Sherbet
Pine Nut Macaroons

A FISH-LOVER'S DINNER

Spinach and Yogurt Soup (*Labenaya*)

◆

Clams or Mussels Marinière, Tyre-style

◆

Baked Stuffed Fish (*Samak Harrah*)
Potatoes with Chick-peas (*Batatas bi Houmus*)

◆

Grapefruit and Avocado Salad

◆

Nut-stuffed Flaky Pastry (*Baklava*)

A CLASSIC LEBANESE SPREAD FOR TEN

Hot Mixed Crushed Nuts (*Muhamara*)
Chick-pea and *Tahini* Dip (*Houmus bi Tahini*)
Egg Plant Dip (*Moutabel*)
Yogurt Cheese Dip (*Labneh*)
All with Arab Bread (*Khoubz*) or pita

◆

Cooked Stuffed Ground Lamb Balls (*Kibbeh bi
Shamiyeh*)
Cooked Cheese on Bread (*Kallaje*)
Broiled Sardines (*Saerdin Mashwi*)
Pickled Vegetables (*Kabbis*)

◆

Cracked Wheat Salad (*Tabbouleh*)
Sweet-Sour Egg Plant (*Bazinjan Rahib*)

◆

Lebanese Shish Kebab (*Lahem Mashwi*)
Garlic Chicken Wings (*Jawaneh*)
Pilau Rice

◆

Yogurt with Honey and Almonds

A SIMPLE FAMILY MEAL

Lebanese Spring Vegetable Soup

◆

Stewed Lamb and Okra (*Bamia Maslu*)
Lentils and Rice (*Mudardara*)

◆

Semolina Cake (*Basboosa*)
Cinnamon Ice Cream

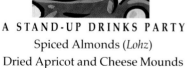

A STAND-UP DRINKS PARTY

Spiced Almonds (*Lohz*)
Dried Apricot and Cheese Mounds
Stuffed Bekkah Radishes
Deep-fried Almond Squid
Spiced Fruit Meatballs with Mint Yogurt Dip
Little Spinach Packets (*Fatayeer*)
Stuffed Fish Balls (*Kibbeh Samak*)
Small Zucchini Puffs (*Aggah bi Kousa*)

SOUPS
SHURBA

CHILLED ARTICHOKE SOUP

SERVES 6

The thistle-like artichoke grows well in the sandier, poorer soils outside the main vegetable-producing Bekkah Valley. In Lebanon, whole small artichokes would be used, but frozen – or even a good brand of canned – artichoke bottoms will do in countries with less profusion!

- ◆ *4 cups chicken stock*
- ◆ *10–12 frozen or canned artichoke bottoms in brine, drained and coarsely chopped*
- ◆ *¾ cup whipping cream*
- ◆ *4 teaspoons lemon juice*
- ◆ *Salt and freshly ground pepper*
- ◆ *Cayenne pepper*
- ◆ *1 small red bell pepper, cored, seeded and finely chopped*
- ◆ *8 scallions, white parts only, finely chopped*

In a large saucepan, combine the stock and the chopped frozen or canned artichokes. Bring to a boil, reduce heat, cover and simmer for about 10 minutes. Remove from the heat and purée in batches in a blender or food processor fitted with a metal blade. Rub the purée through a strainer into a large bowl and allow to cool somewhat. Stir in the cream and lemon juice; add salt, pepper and cayenne to taste. Cover and chill overnight.

Before serving, taste the soup and adjust seasoning, if necessary. Divide the soup among 6 bowls and serve, garnished with a sprinkling of red bell pepper and scallions.

LENTIL SOUP WITH GARLIC AND ONION
SHURIT 'AADS

SERVES 6–8

Lentils are a staple of Lebanese peasant cooking – and of Middle-Eastern cuisine in general. For soups the small red variety are the most often used, since they soften quickly and have a slightly less earthy flavor than other varieties.

- ◆ *8 cups beef or lamb stock*
- ◆ *1 pound red lentils, washed and drained*
- ◆ *2 large onions, chopped*
- ◆ *2 celery stalks, chopped*
- ◆ *1 large beef tomato, peeled, seeded and chopped*
- ◆ *2 tablespoons* samneh
- ◆ *Salt and freshly ground pepper*
- ◆ *1½ teaspoons ground cumin*
- ◆ *1½ teaspoons* Taratoor bi Sade *(page 111)*
- ◆ *Lemon quarters*

In a large saucepan, bring the stock to the boil. Add the lentils, half the onions, the celery and tomato. Bring back to the boil, lower the heat, cover and simmer for about 50 minutes.

Meanwhile, in a small skillet, melt half the *samneh* over a medium heat. Add the remaining onions and sauté gently, stirring continuously, until the onions are soft and caramelized. Take the pan off the heat and reserve.

When the lentils and vegetables are soft, purée the soup in batches in a blender or food processor fitted with a metal blade. Return the soup to the saucepan, add salt and pepper to taste, the cumin, and the *Taratoor*. Reheat for about 5 minutes, stirring. Just before serving, stir in the remaining *samneh*.

Ladle into bowls and garnish each with some of the caramelized onions. Serve with lemon quarters to squeeze into the soup.

CUCUMBER AND CUMIN SOUP

SERVES 6

Perfect for a hot day, this is a Levantine version of a soup popular throughout the Middle East, Turkey and the Balkans.

- ½ teaspoon cumin seed
- 4 cucumbers (about 1 pound, peeled, seeded and chopped
- 2 small garlic cloves, crushed
- 2 cups buttermilk
- Salt and freshly ground pepper
- 6 thin slices lemon

Spread the cumin seeds on a baking sheet, and toast gently under the broiler until lightly colored. Turn the cumin seeds, chopped cucumbers, garlic and buttermilk into a blender or food processor fitted with a metal blade and process until smooth.

Pour the soup into a large bowl, season to taste, and chill for several hours. Serve the soup in bowls, with a thin slice of lemon floating on the top.

SPINACH AND YOGURT SOUP
LABENAYA

SERVES 6

Popular in Egypt, Jordan and Lebanon, this soup is more usually made with beet greens, which impart a characteristic, slightly sour, flavor. When the more easily obtainable spinach is used, as in this recipe, a touch of light white wine vinegar will help to approximate the taste.

- 1 garlic clove, crushed
- 2 cups Greek-style yogurt
- Large pinch turmeric
- 3 tablespoons olive oil
- 1 large onion, finely chopped
- 1 pound spinach leaves, washed thoroughly and shredded
- 2 small leeks, finely chopped
- ¾ cup long-grained rice
- 1 cup vegetable stock
- 3 tablespoons white wine vinegar (champagne vinegar, if available)
- Salt and freshly ground pepper

In a bowl, whisk together the garlic, yogurt and turmeric. Set aside to let the flavors mingle.

Heat the olive oil in a large casserole and stir in the onion. Sauté until lightly colored and softened, then stir in the spinach, leeks and rice. When the spinach has wilted and the rice is coated, pour in the vegetable stock and the vinegar. Season to taste. Bring to the boil, then reduce the heat, cover and simmer for about 15–20 minutes, until the rice is tender.

Just before serving, take the soup off the heat. Whisk in the yogurt mixture, and then ladle immediately into bowls.

LEMON CHICKEN SOUP

SERVES 6

Chickens in the peasant areas are very much free range and, since they are valued for their eggs, can live to a ripe age (for a chicken!). Older hens find their way into soups like this one.

- ◆ 3–4 pound free-range chicken, cut into pieces
- ◆ 2½ cups chicken stock
- ◆ 1 medium onion, chopped
- ◆ 2 large beef tomatoes, peeled, seeded and chopped
- ◆ 1 tablespoon fresh tarragon leaves
- ◆ 1 teaspoon grated lemon peel
- ◆ Salt and freshly ground pepper
- ◆ 2 Cyprus potatoes, peeled and chopped
- ◆ 8 ounces okra, trimmed
- ◆ ½ cup canned chopped jalapeño chilies
- ◆ ¾ cup frozen corn kernels
- ◆ Juice of 1 lemon
- ◆ Chopped flat-leaved parsley
- ◆ Paprika

In a large casserole, combine the chicken pieces (except for the breasts), the stock, onion, tomatoes, tarragon and peel. Pour over 3 cups of water, season to taste, and bring to the boil. Reduce the heat, cover and simmer for 20 minutes. Add the breasts and continue to cook until the breasts are just cooked through. Remove all the chicken pieces from the soup with a slotted spoon and set them aside to cool.

Add the potatoes to the soup, cover and continue to simmer until the potatoes are done, about 25 minutes; add the okra after 10 minutes.

When the chicken is cool enough to handle, remove the meat from the bones, discarding the skin. Chop the meat into small pieces. Add to the soup, together with the chilies and corn kernels. Bring the soup back to the boil, reduce heat, and simmer for 5 more minutes. Stir in the lemon juice and serve immediately, garnished with chopped parsley and paprika to taste.

LEBANESE SPRING VEGETABLE SOUP

SERVES 6

When the fresh spring vegetables come into season – particularly the prized fava bean – they find their way into soups like this one, a version which has been influenced by the Sephardic Jews who have passed through Lebanon.

- ◆ 1 cup chicken stock
- ◆ 1 Spanish onion, finely chopped
- ◆ 2 small garlic cloves, crushed
- ◆ 2 sticks celery, finely chopped
- ◆ Salt and freshly ground pepper
- ◆ 2 leeks, topped, cleaned and thinly sliced into strips
- ◆ 5 artichoke hearts, chopped
- ◆ 1¼ cups shelled fava

- beans (or lima beans, if unavailable)
- ◆ 60 ml/4 tablespoons finely chopped mint
- ◆ 60 ml/4 tablespoons finely chopped coriander
- ◆ 60 ml/4 tablespoons finely chopped flat-leaved parsley
- ◆ Cayenne pepper
- ◆ Pita bread, split in half lengthwise, toasted and torn into shreds

In a large saucepan, combine the chicken stock, onion, garlic cloves, celery and seasoning to taste. Add 1½ cups of water to the pan. Bring the mixture to the boil, then reduce the heat and simmer for about 15 minutes. Add the leeks, artichoke hearts, and fava beans, and simmer for 35 minutes or until the beans are tender. Take off the heat, and stir in the fresh herbs and cayenne to taste.

Allow the herbs to infuse in the soup for a few minutes, then serve with the shredded, toasted pita scattered over the top.

TOMATO AND CORIANDER SOUP

SERVES 6

Coriander is a familiar herb in Lebanese dishes, to which it imparts a tang far more appealing than its rather foetid smell would suggest. This is a summer soup, using the lush tomatoes of the inland valleys, and would make an excellent preliminary to a fish or poultry main dish.

- ◆ 3 pounds ripe, plump tomatoes, roughly chopped
- ◆ 1 small onion
- ◆ ¾ cup tomato juice
- ◆ 3 tablespoons freshly squeezed orange juice
- ◆ 1 Greek or Italian pickled pepper, seeded

- ◆ 4 ml/¾ teaspoon caster sugar
- ◆ Ice water
- ◆ 60 ml/4 tablespoons finely chopped fresh coriander
- ◆ 150 ml/¼ pint Greek-style yogurt

In a blender or food processor fitted with a metal blade, purée the chopped tomatoes and orange juice, pepper and sugar until it is as smooth as possible.

Press the purée through the strainer, rubbing with a wooden spoon to force as much through as possible. Discard the residue, and add enough ice water to thin the purée to a soup-like consistency. Stir in the coriander, cover and chill until cold. Pass the yogurt separately at the table, to allow guests to add as much of it as they wish.

Lebanese Spring Vegetable Soup.

SIDON MELON SOUP
SHURBAT SHAEMAN

SERVES 6

Melons of all types – green, yellow and orange – grow profusely on the small farms of the inland valleys and, until the Middle East crisis, were among the prime exports of the country. When at their peak, they are pleasing simply cut in half or quarters. This ingenious two-tone soup can make use of slightly over-ripe fruit.

- 2 large ogen melons, peeled, seeded and chopped
- 4 tablespoons lime juice
- 4 tablespoons superfine sugar
- 2 large cantaloupe

- melons, peeled, seeded and chopped
- 4 tablespoons lemon juice
- ½ cup Greek-style yogurt
- Ground cinnamon
- Mint leaves

In the bowl of a blender or food processor fitted with a metal blade, purée the ogen melon, lime juice and 2 tablespoons sugar until smooth. Pour into a pitcher, cover and chill until cold.

Rinse out the bowl of the processor or blender and fill with the cantaloupe melon, lemon juice and remaining sugar. Purée until smooth. Pour into a pitcher, cover and chill until cold.

When ready to serve, position each soup bowl in front of you. Pick up both pitchers, and pour the two soups into the bowl at the same time, one on each side. Repeat with the remaining bowls.

Each soup will be two-tone; use a spoon to feather the edges gently to obtain a softer effect. Top each serving with a dollop of yogurt sprinkled lightly with cinnamon and garnished with a sprig of mint.

APPETIZERS, DIPS AND SALADS
MEZE WI SALAT

SPICED NUT MIX
DUKKAH

MAKES 1½ CUPS

This is a traditional Egyptian dish which has made its way around the cusp of the Eastern Mediterranean. There is no hard and fast combination of spices or proportion of nuts – chick-peas are the resort of the poorer households. *Dukkah* is eaten scooped up with Arab bread.

- ¼ *cups shelled hazelnuts or soaked and dried chick-peas*
- *1 cup seasame seeds*
- *1 cup coriander seeds*
- ⅔ *cup cumin seeds*
- *Salt and freshly ground pepper*
- ¼ *teaspoon dried thyme*
- ¼ *teaspoon dried marjoram*
- *Dried lemon peel (optional)*

Heat the oven to 350°F.

Roast the hazelnuts or chick-peas on a baking sheet until golden, about 8 minutes, watching carefully so that they do not burn. Remove and scrape into the bowl of a food processor fitted with a metal blade.

Spread the sesame, coriander and cumin seeds in separate parts of the baking sheet, and roast until they are all colored and toasted, about 5 minutes. Remove and scrape them into the food processor bowl. Add salt and pepper to taste, the thyme, marjoram and lemon peel, if desired. Leave the nuts and seeds to cool to just warm before grinding; otherwise the nut oils will make the mixture too wet. Pulse

briefly on and off until the *dukkah* is roughly ground; do not over-process. Serve with pieces of Arab bread.

The *dukkah* will keep well for about 1 week if stored in an airtight container.

AVOCADO BI TAHINI

MAKES 1¾ CUPS

This is a standard *mezze* when ripe avocados flood the markets in Lebanon, though it is less frequently encountered in Lebanese restaurants abroad. It is particularly simple to make.

- *2 garlic cloves, crushed*
- *Salt*
- *2 ripe avocados*
- *Juice of 2 lemons*
- *5 tablespoons* tahini *paste*
- *1 teaspoon ground cumin*
- *Crushed red chilies*

In a bowl, mash the garlic with salt to taste. Cut the avocados in half, take out the pit, and scoop the flesh into the bowl. Mash together with salt and garlic and a little of the lemon juice, until there are no lumps. Whip in the remaining lemon juice, the *tahini* and the ground cumin. Beat to a smooth purée.

Turn the purée into a bowl, swirl the top decoratively, and rub a few crushed chili peppers between the fingers to sprinkle over the top. Serve with Arab bread (*khoubz*) or pita.

SPICED ALMONDS
LOHZ

MAKES 2½ CUPS

Nuts play a large part in the Levantine diet, and appear as appetizers, in main courses and in desserts. Both spicy and sweet nuts appear as *mezze* or snacks; these almonds are a spicy version.

- ◆ 3 tablespoons sunflower oil
- ◆ 2½ cups whole blanched almond
- ◆ generous 1 cup light brown sugar
- ◆ ½ teaspoon ground cumin
- ◆ 1 teaspoon crushed chili flakes
- ◆ Salt to taste

Heat the oil over a medium-high heat until it is hot. Add the almonds, stirring, together with ¾ of the sugar. Toss the nuts in the sugar to coat thoroughly, and sauté until the nuts are caramelized.

Remove the nuts to a bowl and toss with the cumin, chili flakes and salt to taste. Spread the nuts out on a baking sheet to dry and, while still warm, sprinkle them with a spoonful or so of the remaining sugar to taste. Serve warm or at room temperature.

The nuts will keep for a couple of weeks if they are stored in an airtight container.

SWEET SPICED PISTACHIOS
FOSTU

MAKES 2½ CUPS

This is another version of nutty nibbles, this time with the accent on sweetness.

- 2½ cups shelled, salted pistachios
- ⅔ cup superfine sugar
- 1 teaspoon ground mace
- 1 teaspoon ground cinnamon

Place the nuts in a skillet without any oil, and heat until they are golden, stirring frequently; this will take about 4–5 minutes. Sprinkle over the sugar, then the spices, and continue to stir until the nuts have been caramelized.

Take the nuts off the heat and spoon onto foil or a baking sheet to dry. They will clump together; if desired, break apart when dry.

The nuts will keep for a couple of weeks in an airtight container.

GREEN BEANS IN OLIVE OIL
LOUBIA BI ZEIT

SERVES 6

This is a favorite, homely Lebanese dish, encountered hot, warm or cold – though most usually the latter. It is an old, reliable stand-by – rather like baked beans in our cuisine.

- ◆ *1 pound green or French beans, trimmed and with strings removed, if necessary*
- ◆ *5 tablespoons olive oil*
- ◆ *1 medium onion, finely chopped*
- ◆ *3 garlic cloves, crushed*
- ◆ *7-ounce can plum tomatoes, drained and chopped*
- ◆ *1 crushed dried chili pepper*
- ◆ *Salt and freshly ground pepper*
- ◆ *Cayenne pepper*

Bring a saucepan of water to the boil. Cut the beans into short lengths, about 2 inches, and then add them to the water, cover and simmer for 5 minutes. Drain them thoroughly.

Heat the oil in a skillet and sauté the onion for about 5–6 minutes, until softened but not colored. Add the garlic and stir for another 2 minutes. Stir in the tomatoes, crushed pepper and the beans. Season with salt, pepper and cayenne to taste. Pour into a serving bowl and cool. Serve the dish either at room temperature or chilled.

LEBANESE BREAD SALAD
FATTOUSH

SERVES 6

This is served as an alternative to *tabbouleh* – indeed, it makes a refreshing change when you feel you are suffering from burghul overkill!

- ◆ *2 large khoubz (Arab bread) or pita, toasted*
- ◆ *Juice of 1½ lemons*
- ◆ *1 cucumber, seeded and cubed*
- ◆ *6 scallions, chopped*
- ◆ *1 small green bell pepper, cored, seeded and finely chopped*
- ◆ *4 plum tomatoes, seeded, drained and chopped*
- ◆ *2 garlic cloves, crushed*
- ◆ *1 tablespoon finely chopped flat-leaved parsley*
- ◆ *1 tablespoon finely chopped coriander*
- ◆ *½ cup olive oil*
- ◆ *Salt and freshly ground pepper*

Cut the toasted bread into small pieces, and place in a bowl. Squeeze over the juice from ½ lemon and toss. Set aside for 5 minutes.

In a larger bowl combine all the other ingredients, with salt and pepper to taste. Toss gently, add the bread and additional lemon juice, and combine. Serve the salad immediately.

HOT MIXED CRUSHED NUTS
MUHUMARA

MAKES 2¼ CUPS

This is a thoroughly Lebanese version of mixed nuts, with a surprisingly spicy flavor. It is an acquired taste, but once acquired, often addictive.

◆ *1 cup shelled walnuts, skinned*
◆ *1 cup shelled pine nuts*
◆ *1 tablespoon sunflower oil*
◆ *1 garlic clove, finely chopped*
◆ *10 radishes, trimmed and finely chopped*

◆ *2 small fresh green chilies, seeded and finely chopped*
◆ *4 scallions, finely chopped*
◆ *½ teaspoon sesame oil*
◆ *Cayenne pepper*
◆ *Salt*

With a mortar and pestle, crush the walnuts in batches until they are in very small pieces. Follow with the pine nuts. Reserve. (Alternatively, chop the nuts with a sharp knife, using a rocking motion. Then use a rolling pin to crush the nuts more finely.)

In a skillet, warm the sunflower oil to a medium heat. Add the garlic, chopped radishes and chilies. Sauté for several minutes, making sure the garlic does not burn. Add the nuts, and toss in the oil for a minute or two, then stir in the scallions and the

sesame oil. Stir for 1 minute, season to taste with cayenne pepper and salt; turn into a bowl to cool.

Serve with Arab bread (*khoubz*) or pita.

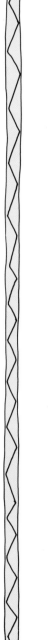

OLIVES BEIRUT-STYLE

Far more varieties and colors of olives are found in the Middle East than make their way to us. Round and torpedo-shaped; green, purple and black; pickled in myriad combinations of brine, vinegars and oils, they are a *mezze* staple. These are lemon-zingy.

◆ *4 tablespoons virgin olive oil*
◆ *2 teaspoons freshly squeezed lemon juice*
◆ *2 cloves of garlic*
◆ *1 teaspoon grated lemon peel*

◆ *½ teaspoon dill seed*
◆ *14-ounce can pitted black or green olives, drained*

In a bowl or jar with a cover, combine the olive oil, lemon juice, garlic, lemon peel and dill seed. Stir thoroughly to combine. Add the olives and agitate to mix well. Cover and chill for 3 days or up to 1 week.

CHEESE BALLS
SHANKLISH

MAKES ABOUT 25–30 BALLS

In Lebanon, these cheese balls would be made of a salted Feta-like goat cheese called *gibna arish*. Here, an unripened *chèvre* log leavened with Feta makes a very acceptable alternative.

- ◆ 8-ounce log unripened chèvre *cheese*
- ◆ 6 ounces Feta cheese
- ◆ *½ teaspoon ground cumin*
- ◆ *¼ teaspoon cayenne pepper*

- ◆ *3 tablespoons finely chopped mint or thyme leaves*
- ◆ *4 tablespoons olive oil*

Combine the cheeses, cumin and cayenne in a bowl and mash together thoroughly. Take out small spoonfuls of cheese and form into bite-sized balls. Roll the balls in the chopped herbs and chill until firm. Before serving, mound the balls on a plate and drizzle the olive oil over them.

APRICOT AND CHEESE MOUNDS

MAKES ABOUT 25 MOUNDS

The influence of the Ashkenazi Jews is evident in the use of poppy seeds in this recipe. For a more Arabic flavor, substitute toasted sesame seeds or pine nuts for the poppy seeds.

- ◆ 1 cup full-fat cream cheese
- ◆ ½ cup shelled and skinned hazelnuts
- ◆ 1 teaspoon freshly ground pepper
- ◆ ½ teaspoon cayenne pepper
- ◆ 25 ready-to-eat dried apricots
- ◆ 4 tablespoons poppy seeds

Preheat the oven to 350°.

Unwrap the cream cheese into a bowl and work until creamy. Spread the hazelnuts on a baking sheet, and toast for about 8 minutes, or until toasted. Remove, chop roughly and stir into the cheese. Season with the pepper and cayenne and combine thoroughly.

Lay out the dried apricots and divide the mixture between them. Form each into a smooth mound. Roll the tops of the mounds in the poppy seeds to coat, then chill for 2–3 hours, until firm.

STUFFED BEKKAH RADISHES

MAKES ABOUT 35 RADISHES

Plump French-style radishes grown in the valleys are a popular hors-d'œuvre in Beirut. But the method of presentation is unashamedly Middle-Eastern.

◆ *1 pound radishes*
◆ *½ cup cream cheese or Labneh (page 53)*
◆ *1 tablespoon capers, chopped*
◆ *¾ cup bottled Kalamata olive purée, drained*

◆ *1½ tablespoons finely chopped flat-leaved parsley*
◆ *Flat-leaved parsley sprigs*

Trim the radishes, so that they will stand on either end. Cut the radishes in half and drop them into a bowl of ice water to crisp. One at a time, using a sharp knife or a melon-baller, hollow out a small hole in each half. Return to the ice water until all the radishes are done. Remove and drain upside down on paper towels.

In a bowl, beat together the cheese, capers, olive purée and chopped parsley until thoroughly combined. Either pipe the filling into the halves or carefully fill with a small spoon and shape the filling with a fork. Garnish each radish with a parsley sprig.

HOUMUS

MAKES ABOUT 2 CUPS

This is a light, fresh version of houmus, without the strong flavor of sesame. It is more lemony and spicy; the Lebanese often serve it with a sprinkling of ground fried lamb.

- ◆ 15-ounce can chick-peas in brine, rinsed and drained
- ◆ 2 garlic cloves, crushed
- ◆ 2 tablespoons olive oil
- ◆ 1 tablespoon sunflower oil
- ◆ 3 tablespoons freshly squeezed lemon juice
- ◆ Salt and freshly ground pepper
- ◆ ½ teaspoon cayenne pepper
- ◆ ¼ teaspoon ground chili
- ◆ 2 tablespoons chopped parsley
- ◆ 4 ounces ground lamb or beef, fried with a little salt, pepper and cinnamon (optional)

In the bowl of a food processor fitted with a metal blade, combine the chickpeas, garlic and olive oil. Process until almost smooth, stopping to push down the paste from the sides of the bowl; then add the sunflower oil, lemon juice, seasoning to taste, spices and parsley. Process until very smooth, adding a little water if you wish a thinner consistency. Scrape into a bowl and swirl decoratively. Serve with Arab bread (*khoubz*) or pita.

If desired, before serving, make a small well in the center of the *houmus* and mound in the cinnamon-fried meat. This should be scooped up with the bread, together with the *houmus*.

HOUMUS BI TAHINI

MAKES ABOUT 2 CUPS

This is the more usual version of _houmus_ found from Greece and Turkey to Egypt. The sesame lends a smokier flavor lacking in the previous version.

- ◆ _15-ounce can chick-peas, rinsed and drained_
- ◆ _1 garlic clove, crushed_
- ◆ _3 tablespoons_ tahini _paste_
- ◆ _1 teaspoon cumin_
- ◆ _2 tablespoons olive oil_
- ◆ _3 tablespoons freshly squeezed lemon juice_
- ◆ _Salt and freshly ground pepper_
- ◆ _Paprika_

In the bowl of a food processor with a metal blade, combine the chick-peas, garlic, _tahini_ paste, cumin and 1 tablespoon olive oil. Process until finely chopped, push the paste down the side of the bowl, add the lemon juice, and salt and pepper to taste and process until the mixture is smooth.

Turn the purée into a bowl, smooth and swirl the surface, and drizzle with the remaining 1 tablespoon olive oil. Sprinkle with paprika, and serve with Arab bread (_khoubz_) or pita.

COLD EGG PLANT PURÉE
MOUTABEL

MAKES ABOUT 2 CUPS

Also called _Baba Ghannoj_ by the Arabs, this dip combines two smoky flavors: that of the broiled egg plant and that of the _tahini_ or sesame paste. It is one of the most popular Lebanese _mezze_ with foreigners, having made its way into the delicatessen department of many supermarkets.

- ◆ _2 medium egg plant, cut in half_
- ◆ _Juice of 1 lemon_
- ◆ _2 garlic cloves, crushed_
- ◆ _3 tablespoons_ tahini
- ◆ _½ teaspoon ground cumin_
- ◆ _Salt and freshly ground pepper_
- ◆ _1 tablespoon flat-leaved parsley_
- ◆ _Black olives_

Prick the skins of the halved egg plant and place them flesh down on a greased baking sheet. Place them under a hot broiler and broil for about 15–20 minutes, rearranging, if necessary, until the skins are blackened and blistered and the flesh is soft. Remove them from the oven, plunge them into cold water, then skin thoroughly, cutting off the skin if it sticks.

Roughly chop the egg plant flesh, and put it into the bowl of a food processor fitted with a metal blade. Add the freshly squeezed lemon juice and process for a few seconds, until combined. Scrape the mixture down the sides of the bowl and add the _tahini_, cumin, and salt and pepper to taste. Process the mixture until it becomes a smooth purée.

Turn the purée into a bowl, cover and chill slightly. Before serving, swirl the top attractively and sprinkle with the chopped parsley and a few black olives. Serve with Arab bread (_khoubz_) or pita.

Stuffed Vine Leaves.

STUFFED VINE LEAVES
WARAH INAB

MAKES 30–50 STUFFED VINE LEAVES

Stuffed vine leaves are popular all over the eastern Mediterranean crescent, from Greece to Egypt. Unlike some of these nationalities, however, the Lebanese prefer their stuffing without meat and served cold.

- 6-ounce packet vine leaves (about 35)
- 4 tablespoons olive oil
- 2 tablespoons pine nuts
- 1 large onion, finely chopped
- ⅓ cup long-grain rice
- Salt and pepper
- 1 tablespoon raisins
- 1½ tablespoons finely chopped mint
- ½ tablespoon cinnamon
- Juice of 2 lemons

Remove the vine leaves from the packet, separate them, place in a large container and pour boiling water over them. Allow to soak for 15 minutes, then drain. Return to the bowl, pour cold water on them, soak for a further 10 minutes, then drain thoroughly on paper towels.

Heat tablespoon of the olive oil in a large skillet. Add the pine nuts and sauté, stirring, for about 4 minutes, or until the nuts are golden. Remove the pine nuts with a slotted spoon and reserve. Add another 1 tablespoon of oil to the pan, and stir in the onions. Sauté until limp and lightly colored, about 5–6 minutes, then add the rice and salt to taste. Stir the rice until it is coated with the oil, then pour in ½ cup boiling water to cover. Reduce the heat, cover, and cook over medium heat for about 5 minutes. Take off the heat and allow to sit until the water has been absorbed, and the rice is tender – about 20 minutes. Stir in the raisins, pine nuts, chopped mint and cinnamon.

Lay a vine leaf flat, and spoon 2 tablespoons of the rice mixture near the stem end. Roll the leaf one turn over the mixture, then tuck in the sides of the leaf toward the center. Contnue to roll the leaf like a cigar, until you reach the end. Squeeze the bundle to remove excess moisture. Repeat the process with the remaining leaves and stuffing.

If there are any vine leaves left over, lay them on the bottom of a lightly oiled casserole. Arrange the stuffed leaves in a single layer on top. Pour over the lemon juice and just enough hot water to cover. Drizzle over the remaining 2 tablespoons olive oil. Weigh the stuffed leaves down with a plate. Cover tightly and cook over high heat for about 4 minutes, then lower the heat and simmer for about 40 minutes. Remove from the heat, uncover and allow to cool in the cooking liquid. When cold, remove the stuffed leaves with a slotted spoon and arrange on a platter.

Serve at room temperature or chilled, together with lemon wedges to squeeze over.

TOMATO AND OLIVE SALAD
SALAT TOMATIN WI ZATUN

SERVES 4–6

This simple salad is a common accompaniment to grills and kebabs. Usually served with a classic vinaigrette or squeeze of lemon juice, it is especially good with Cumin-Lemon Dressing.

- 5–6 large tomatoes, cored and cut into thin slices
- 1 large red onion, finely chopped
- 1 cup pitted black olives
- 4 tablespoons finely chopped flat-leaved parsley
- Salt and pepper
- ½ cup Cumin-Lemon Dressing (page 108)

Lay the sliced tomatoes on a serving platter, and scatter over the chopped onion and then the olives and parsley. Season with salt and pepper to taste. Pour over the dressing or lemon juice and serve the salad immediately.

RAW LAMB MIXED WITH SPICES
KIBBEH NAYEH

SERVES 6–8

This Lebanese version of steak tartare, made with lamb instead of beef and extended by the addition of burghul, is an adventure in taste worth experiencing. However, the lamb must be of exceedingly good quality and very tender. This version is traditionally served on a glass platter surrounded with cos lettuce leaves for scooping up the *kibbeh,* like edible spoons. When the mixture is rolled into balls it is called *kibbeh orayeh.*

- ◆ *1 pound tender lean lamb (tenderloin or leg), finely chopped*
- ◆ *Salt and freshly ground pepper*
- ◆ *1 large onion, chopped*
- ◆ *1½ cups fine-ground burghul*
- ◆ *½ teaspoon ground allspice*
- ◆ *1 teaspoon ground cumin*
- ◆ *Cayenne pepper*
- ◆ *Olive oil*
- ◆ *5 scalllions, finely chopped*
- ◆ *Cos lettuce or chicory leaves (optional)*

Put the pieces of lamb into the bowl of a food processor fitted with a metal blade. Process until roughly ground, then add salt and pepper to taste, along with the chopped onion. Process the mixture, stopping to scrape down the sides of the bowl, until it is a smooth paste. Turn into a large bowl.

Place the burghul in another bowl, and cover with cold water. Allow to soak for about 5 minutes. Turn the cracked wheat into a strainer lined with muslin or a fine cloth and allow to drain for a few minutes. Pull together the ends of the muslin and squeeze out the remaining moisture. Turn the burghul into the bowl with the meat.

Sprinkle over the allspice and cumin, and add cayenne to taste. Using moistened hands, work the burghul and lamb together, kneading and pressing, until you have a grainy paste. This will take about 5 minutes. Leave for about half an hour.

If you are serving the meat as *kibbeh orayeh,* form it into small, walnut-sized balls or flatten into little patties. If you are serving *kibbeh nayeh,* together with the cos leaves, then add 1–2 teaspoons water, and knead the paste further in order to give it a more mousse-like consistency.

Pile the *kibbeh* onto a platter. Before serving the balls, drizzle over the olive oil. With the *kibbeh nayeh,* serve the oil separately, for guests to add as they wish. Decorate both platters with a sprinkling of chopped scallion and lemon wedges.

MINT AND SWEET LEAF SALAD

SERVES 4–6

A contrast to the salad on page 44, this is a combination of delicate young greens and a tart oil-and-lemon dressing.

- ◆ *½ cup lemon juice*
- ◆ *½ cup olive oil*
- ◆ *Salt and freshly ground pepper*
- ◆ *1 small head butter lettuce, washed, dried and divided into leaves*
- ◆ *1 small head oak-leaved lettuce, washed, dried and divided into leaves*
- ◆ *2 ounces whole mint leaves, washed and dried*

In a serving bowl, whisk together the lemon juice, oil and seasoning until combined. Add the lettuce leaves and mint leaves, and toss gently to coat. Serve the salad immediately.

LITTLE SPINACH PACKETS
FATAYEER

MAKES ABOUT 25 PASTRIES

Made with the same dough as the *Lahem* (page 44), these can be filled with a cheese mixture (see *Sambousek* filling, page 48), meat, or this sour spinach mixture, probably the most typical. Such Levantine stuffed pastries were the prototypes of the Cornish pasties and meat pies which developed in Britain after the Crusades.

◆ *1 portion* lahme *dough, chilled for 30 minutes (page 44)*

FILLING
◆ *2 pounds fresh leaf spinach, washed, de-stems removed, drained and chopped*
◆ *3 tablespoons olive oil*
◆ *1 onion, grated*

◆ *Seeds of 1 pomegranate*
◆ *1 cup walnuts, crushed*
◆ *1 tablespoon sumac (optional)*
◆ *Juice of 1½ lemons*
◆ *Salt and freshly ground pepper*

Squeeze as much moisture as possible from the spinach. In a skillet, heat the oil and stir in the grated onion. Cook for 2 minutes, then add the spinach and stir until the spinach is thoroughly wilted. Add the seeds of the pomegranate, walnuts, sumac, if wished, and the lemon juice. Combine well, then take off the heat and set aside.

Break off the dough into 25 pieces and form into balls. On a floured board, roll the balls into small circles as thin as possible. Divide the filling among the circles. Place the filling in the center of each circle, and bring up the sides to form three-sided packets. Pinch the top edges together.

Preheat the oven to 375°.

Place the pastries on oiled baking sheets, and bake for 5 minutes. Then lower the heat to 350° and continue baking for a further 15–20 minutes. Remove from the oven and let them cool slightly before serving warm.

COOKED STUFFED GROUND LAMB BALLS

KIBBEH BI SHAMIYEH

MAKES ABOUT 20 STUFFED *KIBBEH*

These plump little shapes, made from cracked wheat and lamb, and stuffed with yet more lamb, are the signature dish of the Lebanese table and are still considered the test of the accomplished housewife. In a country where the food processor remains a rarity, the paste-like outer shell requires dedicated pounding in mortar and pestle, and careful treatment in stuffing and cooking to withstand breakage. We in the West have an easier time of it.

◆ *1 pound lean tender lamb (leg or tenderloin), finely chopped*

◆ *1 large onion, chopped*

◆ *2–2½ cups fine-ground burghul*

◆ *Cayenne pepper*

◆ *1 teaspoon cumin*

◆ *5 ml/1 tsp cumin*

FILLING

◆ *2 tablespoons olive oil*

◆ *2 tablespoons pine nuts*

◆ *2 small onions, finely chopped*

◆ *8 ounces ground lamb*

◆ *1 tablespoon Lebanese spice (page 16)*

◆ *Salt and freshly ground pepper*

◆ *Oil for deep-frying*

◆ *Lemon wedges*

Put the small pieces of lamb in the bowl of a food processor fitted with a metal blade. Process until roughly ground, then add the chopped onion. Continue to process, stopping once or twice to scrape the mixture down the sides of the bowl, until the meat has become a smooth paste. Turn from the food processor into a large bowl.

Place 2½ cups burghul in another bowl and cover with cold water. Allow to soak for about 10 minutes. Turn the burghul into a strainer lined with muslin or a fine cloth, and allow to drain for a few minutes. Pull together the ends of the muslin and thoroughly squeeze out the remaining moisture. Turn most of the burghul into the bowl containing the meat, reserving less than a quarter.

Sprinkle cayenne pepper to taste and the cumin over the meat and burghul. Using moistened hands, work the grain and lamb together, kneading and pressing, until it is a fine paste that will take a firm shape. Work in some of the reserved burghul, if necessary. Chill for 30 minutes–1 hour.

Meanwhile make the filling. Heat the oil in a skillet and sauté the pine nuts for about 2 minutes, until browned slightly. Remove the nuts with a slotted spoon and reserve.

Stir in the chopped onion and sauté for about 5–6 minutes until limp and just coloring. Add the ground lamb and the spice and fry until the meat is browned. Remove from the heat, drain off the excess fat, seäson to taste and stir in the pine nuts. Set aside.

Divide the *kibbeh* "dough" into about 20 pieces. Roll the pieces between your palms to form egg shapes. Take one "egg" and, using your index finger, make a hole from one end toward the center, pressing and shaping the "dough" to make a largish hole with the shell as thin as possible. Fill the hole with some of the lamb filling, then pinch the open end shut, sealing in the filling. Tease the *kibbeh* into an oval with pointed ends. Repeat the stuffing process with the remaining "egg" shells and filling.

Heat the oil for frying in a large heavy saucepan or deep-fryer. Deep-fry in batches, until the *kibbeh* become a deep golden brown. Drain on paper towels.

Serve on a large platter with lemon wedges. The *kibbeh* can be refrigerated or frozen, and reheated in the oven when needed.

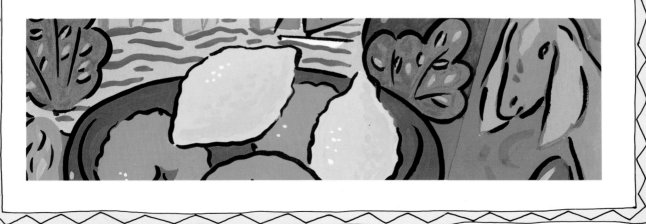

LEBANESE LAMB PIZZA
LAHEM BIL AJINE

MAKES ABOUT 25 BITE-SIZED PIZZAS

This typically Lebanese open-faced pie uses a yeast bread dough, which produces a rather floppy version of pizza. The same dough is also used to make the *fatayeer* in the recipe on page 41. Although lamb is the traditional meat to use, the pizzas can also be made with ground beef.

- 3 cups lukewarm water
- 4 ounces fresh yeast or ½ teaspoon dry yeast
- 4 cups flour
- 1 teaspoon salt
- 1½–2 tablespoons olive oil
- Olive oil (for coating)

TOPPING
- 2 tablespoons olive oil
- 1 pound mild onions, finely chopped
- 1 pound ground lamb

- 14-ounce can chopped chili tomatoes, well drained
- ¾ cup tomato paste
- 1 teaspoon Lebanese spice
- 1 teaspoon brown sugar
- Salt and freshly ground pepper
- 1 tablespoon finely chopped coriander
- 1 tablespoon finely chopped parsley

In a bowl, stir together half the water and yeast. Leave to rest for 15 minutes, or until mixture begins to foam.

In another bowl, sift together the flour and the salt. Make a well in the middle and pour in the oil, then the yeast mixture. Using your hands, pull the flour into the liquid and begin to work into a dough. Add the remaining lukewarm water little by little to incorporate fully. When all the water has been added and the dough sticks together, remove from the bowl. On a lightly floured surface knead the dough well, for about 15 minutes, until it becomes shiny and elastic, about 15 minutes. Pat the dough into a ball.

Pour a little oil in the bowl, place the dough in it and turn the ball to coat it. Remove the ball to a warm place and cover with a damp cloth. Leave for about 2½ hours, until it has doubled in size.

To make the filling, heat the oil in a skillet and add the onions. Sauté until limp and lightly colored. In a bowl, combine the meat, well-drained tomatoes, tomato paste, spice, sugar, salt and pepper to taste, and the herbs. Add the cooked onions and mix the ingredients using the hands.

With dampened hands, break off pieces of the dough and form into 25 balls. Press each ball between the hands, flattening into a small disc, and place on an oiled baking sheet. Divide the topping between the pizza bases, spreading evenly. Bake in a preheated oven at 425°, for about 10 minutes, until a little puffy and lightly colored. Remove from the oven and serve immediately.

The *lahem* can be refrigerated or frozen and reheated in the oven when needed.

MIXED BITTER LEAF SALAD

SERVES 4–6

Taking their cue from the biblical reference to bitter herbs, this salad has a palate-awakening effect. The addition of Pistachio Dressing, however, makes the result far more lip-smacking.

Arrange the chicory leaves around the edges of a shallow serving bowl. In the center, mix together the cos lettuce and watercress. Pour over the Pistachio Dressing, toss gently and serve immediately.

- 2 medium heads chicory, rinsed, dried and broken into leaves
- 15 inner leaves of cos lettuce, rinsed, dried, broken into leaves and roughly chopped
- 1 bunch watercress, washed, dried and with excess stems removed
- ¾ cup Pistachio Dressing (page 109)

SPICED FRUIT MEATBALLS

MAKES 25–30 BALLS

Mouth-watering meatballs such as these occur in many variations throughout the Middle East. The inclusion of fruit is a preference of Turkey and the Levant, where the mingling of savory and sweet is more common. Currants or dates can be substituted for the white raisins. This goes particularly well with Yogurt Sauce (page 108).

- ◆ scant 1 cup fresh white bread crumbs
- ◆ ½ cup yogurt
- ◆ 3 tablespoons olive oil
- ◆ ½ cup pine nuts
- ◆ ⅓ cup white raisins, soaked in hot water and drained
- ◆ 3 tablespoons finely chopped scallions
- ◆ 1 clove garlic, finely chopped
- ◆ 1 teaspoon ground cinnamon
- ◆ 1 teaspoon ground allspice
- ◆ 1 teaspoon salt
- ◆ 1 pound ground lamb or beef
- ◆ 1 tablespoon oil

In a bowl, mix together the bread crumbs and yogurt and leave to soak for 10 minutes. In a skillet heat 1 tablespoon of the oil, and sauté the pine nuts until lightly golden, about 4–5 minutes. Drain on paper towels and add to the yogurt mix.

Stir in the white raisins, scallion, garlic, spices and salt. Add the meat and combine thoroughly using your hands. Chill the meat mixture for 30 minutes.

Make about 30 small balls from the mixture. Heat the oil and sauté the balls in batches for about 6 minutes, turning to ensure they brown all over. Transfer to paper towels to drain, and keep warm while cooking the remaining balls.

The balls may be refrigerated or frozen and reheated in the oven when required.

ANCHOVY AND EGG FRITTERS
AGGAH BI ANSHUGA

SERVES 6–8

Eggah, as it is known in Egypt where it is particularly popular, occurs in a number of guises throughout the region. A form of omelet, it is sometimes made with flour in Lebanon, becoming a *beignet.* Here it is extended with potato and cut into wedges.

◆ 2 tablespoons olive or
   sunflower oil
◆ 5 scallions, finely
   chopped
◆ 6 anchovies, washed,
   drained, dried and
   finely chopped
◆ 1 large potato, grated

◆ 1 teaspoon cumin
◆ 3 tablespoons finely
   chopped flat-leaved
   parsley
◆ 6 eggs
◆ Salt and freshly ground
   pepper

Heat the oil in a large skillet with a cover. When hot, add the chopped scallion and sauté until they are limp. Take off the heat and remove the scallion with a slotted spoon to a large bowl.

Add the chopped anchovy, grated potato, cumin and parsley to the bowl, and mix together. One by one, beat in the eggs. Season according to taste.

Put the pan back on the heat, turning to coat it with the oil. Pour in the egg mixture, turn the heat to low, and cover. Cook for about 15–20 minutes, until the eggs are just set.

Uncover the pan, put a plate over the top, and invert the flat omelet onto the plate. Carefully slip back into the pan and cook for a further 3 minutes.

Remove the omelet, cut into thin wedges, and roll up each wedge, fat end to thin point of the triangle. Secure with a toothpick. Serve warm or cold.

SPICED CHICK-PEA BALLS
FALAFEL

MAKES ABOUT 25–30 BALLS

Although most closely associated with Israel, *falafel* are eaten all over the Middle East and appear on every Lebanese restaurant menu. The *falafel* can be made using only bread (and no burghul), which gives them a denser consistency.

- ◆ *3 ounces Arab bread (khoubz) or pita, torn into shreds*
- ◆ *¾ cup fine-ground burghul*
- ◆ *14-ounce can chick-peas, rinsed and drained*
- ◆ *3 garlic cloves, crushed*
- ◆ *1 small onion, chopped*
- ◆ *1 teaspoon crushed red*
- ◆ *pepper, flaked*
- ◆ *2 teaspoons chopped coriander*
- ◆ *1 teaspoon lemon juice*
- ◆ *1 teaspoon ground cumin*
- ◆ *Salt and freshly ground pepper*
- ◆ *Oil for deep frying*

In a small bowl, combine the shredded bread with water to cover. Leave for about 15 minutes. In another bowl, combine the burghul with water to cover. Leave for 15 minutes also.

Meanwhile, in the bowl of a food processor fitted with a metal blade, combine the drained chick-peas, the garlic, onion, spices and lemon juice. Process, stopping to push the paste down the sides of the bowl, until it is smooth.

Drain the bread and the burghul. Squeeze both as dry as possible, separately, in muslin or a fine cloth. Add the bread to the chick-pea paste and process until it is as smooth as possible.

Scrape the paste into a bowl. Add the burghul, season with salt and pepper to taste, and thoroughly combine the mixture with the hands. Shape into small nut-sized balls, arrange on greaseproof paper and chill – in layers if necessary – for about 2 hours.

Heat the oil in a deep-fryer or saucepan until just smoking at about 375°. Deep-fry the balls for about 4 minutes each, until golden brown. Drain the balls on paper towels.

Serve the *felafel* warm with *Taratoor bi Tahini* (page 106) or Yogurt and Cucumber Sauce (page 108).

COOKED CHEESE WITH BREAD
KALLAJE

MAKES 12 ROUNDS

This is an adaptation of the plain grilled cheese on toasted pita served at Lebanese, Greek and Turkish restaurants, which is often unappetizingly rubbery and lacking in any taste other than that of salt. This version allows the distinctive flavors of the region to assert themselves.

- ◆ *3 tablespoons semnah or butter, melted*
- ◆ *6 fresh pita or pocket bread*
- ◆ *1½ pounds Kasseri or Hallomi cheese, grated*
- ◆ *1 garlic clove, finely chopped*
- ◆ *1 teaspoon fresh marjoram, finely chopped*
- ◆ *½ cup fresh lemon juice*

Lightly brush two muffin pans with some of the melted *semnah* or butter. From each pita, cut two circles of bread to fit two muffin cups. Repeat with the remaining pitas. Place a bread circle in each muffin cup and brush with the remaining *semnah*.

In a bowl, mix together the cheese, garlic, marjoram and lemon juice. Take handfuls of the mixture and top the pita rounds with it.

Place the muffin pans in an oven preheated to 400°, and bake for about 10 minutes, or until the cheese is bubbling and slightly browned. Serve immediately.

LAMB CRESCENT PASTRIES
LAMB SAMBOUSEK

MAKES ABOUT 25 PASTRIES

The following recipe includes a traditional meat filling. The cheese filling used in the savory *baklava* could be used instead, omitting the tomatoes and substituting 2–3 tablespoons dill or mint.

◆ *1½ cups flour*
◆ *Salt*
◆ *1 tablespoon sunflower oil*
◆ *1 onion, finely chopped*
◆ *1 garlic clove, finely chopped*
◆ *12 ounces ground lamb*
◆ *2 tablespoons pine nuts*
◆ *Salt and freshly ground*
◆ *black pepper*
◆ *1 tablespoon Lebanese spice (page 16)*
◆ *2 tablespoons chopped mint*
◆ *1 teaspoon sugar*
◆ *2 tablespoons lemon juice*
◆ *1 egg, beaten*
◆ *Oil for deep-frying*
◆ *½ cup warm water*

Sift the flour, salted to taste, into a bowl. Slowly add the water, mixing with a knife. Then work with the hands and remove from the bowl. Knead on a floured surface for 5 minutes, until smooth. Wrap in plastic wrap and chill for 30 minutes.

In a skillet heat the oil and sauté the onion and garlic until limp and lightly colored. Stir in the ground lamb, and cook until browned all over. Drain off the excess fat. Add the pine nuts, salt and pepper to taste, the spice and mint, and the sugar. Cook for a further 2–3 minutes, then take off the heat. Stir in the lemon juice.

To make the pastries, divide the dough into about 25 little balls. Roll out one on a floured board into a small circle, spoon a little of the filling into the center of the circle, dampen the edges with a little beaten egg, and fold the pastry over the filling. Crimp the edges with a fork. Repeat the process with the remaining balls and filling.

Heat the oil for deep-frying. When it has reached 375°, drop the pastries in, 3–4 at a time. Cook until golden brown and remove with a slotted spoon onto paper towels to drain. Bring the oil back to the correct heat, and continue until all the pastries have been fried (adding a little more oil when necessary). Keep warm until ready to serve.

The pastries may be refrigerated or frozen after frying. They can be reheated in the oven when needed.

A modern restaurant by an old bridge, Jezir El Khadi.

SAVOURY BAKLAVA

SERVES 6

This mouth-watering cheese-and-onion pie makes a delicious hors-d'œuvre at a drinks party, on its own or paired with *Kibbeg bi Sanieh.* The sun-dried tomato is a new introduction from Italian residents of Lebanon, but it marries wonderfully with the cheese. The *baklava* can be served cold, but is at its best warm – not piping hot.

- ¾ cup samneh (page 14) or butter
- 2 onions, finely chopped
- 2 garlic cloves, finely chopped
- ¼ teaspoon dry marjoram
- ¼ teaspoon dry thyme
- 8 ounces Feta cheese
- 1 cup Labneh (page 53)
- 2 eggs
- 2 tablespoons milk
- 2 ounces sun-dried tomatoes in oil, drained and finely chopped
- Salt and freshly ground pepper
- 8 ounces phyllo pastry (in 8 × 12 inch sheets)

In a skillet, warm 2 tablespoons of the *smenah* or butter. Add the onions and sauté, for about 5 minutes, stirring throughout. Add the garlic and herbs, and continue to cook until the onions are limp and lightly colored. Scrape into a bowl.

Add the two cheeses and the eggs to the onion mixture, beating to combine. Stir in the milk, then the sun-dried tomatoes and seasoning to taste. Continue to beat until everything is well mixed.

Melt the remaining *smenah* or butter carefully over medium heat. Unwrap the phyllo sheets and cover them with a wet cloth to prevent drying while making the *baklava.* Brush the bottom of a shallow baking sheet or pan with butter. (It should be large enough just to accommodate the phyllo sheets. If slightly smaller, overlap the edges of the pastry as you "build" the pie.) Lay two sheets of phyllo in the pan and brush with the melted *smenah.* Lay two more sheets on top and brush with more *smenah.* Continue until you have used half the phyllo.

Spread the cheese filling evenly over the pastry. Cover with two sheets of phyllo, brush with *smenah,* and add two more sheets. Continue as before, until you have used all the phyllo. Brush the top generously with the *smenah,* and cut the pie into bite-sized diamond-shaped pieces.

Bake in an oven preheated to 400° for about 45 minutes, or until the top is golden and the filling cooked. Allow to cool slightly, then re-cut the *baklava* and serve it.

LEBANESE COLESLAW
SALAT MALFOOF

SERVES 6–8

This cabbage salad has a strong garlic flavor, and complements grills and barbecued meats wonderfully.

- 2 garlic cloves
- 1 teaspoon salt
- ½ cup fresh lemon juice
- ½ cup olive oil
- 1 small Dutch white cabbage (about 12 ounces), cored and shredded
- 3 tablespoons fresh mint, shredded
- 3 tablespoons caraway seeds

Using a mortar and pestle, mash the garlic with the salt until you have a paste. Slowly work in the lemon juice. Transfer the sauce to a large bowl and whisk in the olive oil adding only a small amount at a time, until the dressing is emulsified.

Add the shredded cabbage, mint and caraway seeds, and fold into the dressing. Serve immediately.

DEEP-FRIED ALMOND SQUID

MAKES ABOUT 25 RINGS

Squid is another favorite of all Mediterranean peoples, and the Lebanese are no exception. This *meze* is lovely and crunchy and is especially well complemented by a dip of Almond Sauce (page 95).

- ◆ 1 pound squid bodies, cleaned, rinsed and patted dry
- ◆ ¾ cup flour
- ◆ Salt and freshly ground pepper
- ◆ Cayenne pepper
- ◆ ¾ cup fine-ground burghul, soaked and drained in a lined strainer overnight
- ◆ ½ cup finely chopped blanched almonds
- ◆ 2 eggs
- ◆ Oil for deep-frying

With a sharp knife, slice the squid sacs into rings and reserve.

Measure the flour onto a plate, and mix in salt, pepper and a little ground cayenne to taste. On another plate put the burghul, which should now be dry. Stir the chopped almonds into the burghul. Crack the eggs into a shallow bowl and beat quickly.

Take the squid rings one by one and dust them with the flour. Then dip the rings into the beaten egg and, finally, coat with the burghul-almond mixture. Place the rings in a single layer on a platter or tray and chill for 1 hour.

Heat the oil to 360°, and deep-fry the rings in batches until golden. Keep warm until served.

STUFFED FISH BALLS
KIBBEH SAMAK

MAKES ABOUT 20 BALLS

In the coastal ports of Sidon and Tyre, tasty alternatives to lamb *kibbeh* take the form of deep-fried fish patties and balls. This is one variation with a light, fruity filling.

- 1 pound fine-ground burghul
- 1 large onion, chopped
- 1½ pounds white fish fillets, skinned
- 2 tablespoons lemon juice
- Salt and freshly ground pepper

FILLING
- 1 large onion, finely chopped
- 1 tablespoon oil
- 3 tablespoons finely chopped coriander
- ⅓ cup chopped ready-to-eat dried apricots
- 2 tablespoons finely chopped dates

- Oil for deep-frying
- Lemon wedges
- Ice water

Put the burghul in a bowl and cover with cold water. Leave for 10 minutes.

Put the chopped onion in the bowl of a food processor fitted with a metal blade. Process until the onion has been thoroughly chopped, then add the fish fillets, and continue to process until the fish is a

Stuffed fish balls

paste. Add the lemon juice and seasoning to the processor, and blend until you have a smooth purée.

Drain the burghul in a strainer lined with muslin or a fine cloth. Then take up the end of the cloth and twist it to squeeze out all the excess moisture. Add the dried burghul in batches to the fish purée, processing between additions. You should end up with a workable dough. If necessary, add a little ice water to make it more malleable.

To make the filling, fry the onion in the oil until it is lightly colored and limp. Stir in the coriander, chopped apricots and chopped dates. Take off the heat and reserve.

With moistened hands, divide the fish dough into about 20 pieces and roll them into balls. Using your index finger, make a hole in each ball and stuff with a little of the filling. Re-form the ball around the filling and pat into shape.

Heat the oil for deep-frying, and drop the fish balls into it a few at a time. Fry until the balls are golden, and remove to paper towels to drain. Serve warm or at room temperature with lemon wedges. They can be refrigerated or frozen and reheated, if necessary.

The *kibbeh* are also delicious dipped into *Taratoor bi Tahini* (page 106) or Yogurt Sauce (page 108).

YOGURT CREAM CHEESE DIP
LABNEH

MAKES ABOUT ½ CUPS

Usually made with goat's milk yogurt in Lebanon, this mild but flavorful cream cheese dip is ubiquitous on the Lebanese table. It is a popular *meze* dip and can be turned into a more substantial variation by the addition of one or more of the following ingredients: chopped cucumber, scallions, sweet peppers or chilies.

- 4 cups plain yogurt (goat or sheep preferred)
- 1 teaspoon salt
- 1 tablespoon olive oil
- Paprika

In a bowl, combine the yogurt and the salt, and whip to mix thoroughly. Line a strainer with damp muslin or a clean, fine-weave cloth. Let it drain in this position for a while, then tie the corners of the cloth together and hang it from a faucet over the sink for about 12 hours or overnight.

To serve, decant the drained cheese into a bowl. Swirl the top decoratively and drizzle the olive oil over the cheese. Sprinkle with the paprika. Serve with Arab bread (*khoubz*) or pita.

RICE AND PISTACHIO SALAD

SERVES 6

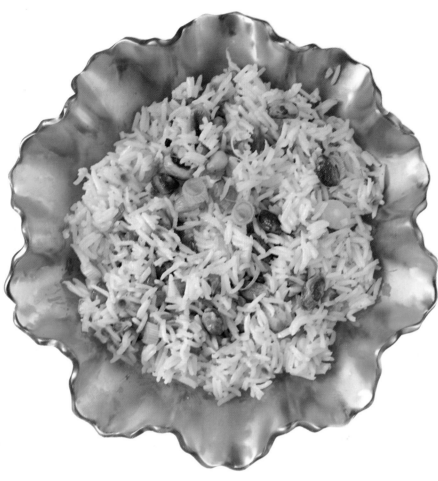

This salad is a visitor – from the eastern borders and Iran – that came to stay. Rice is very much a secondary grain in Lebanon; a refinement of Beirut and the larger towns, which can boast a more cosmopolitan clientele than the masses who rely on burghul. (This salad is exceptionally delicious made with 4 tablespoons pistachio oil substituted for the olive oil used to toss the salad. It can be obtained in some delicatessens, but is unfortunately very expensive.)

◆ 2 cups long-grain rice
◆ 5 tablespoons olive oil
◆ Salt and freshly ground pepper
◆ 3 tablespoons fresh lemon juice
◆ 1 teaspoon grated lemon peel
◆ 1 teaspoon pomegranate seeds
◆ 3 tablespoons finely chopped flat-leaved parsley
◆ 4 scallions, finely chopped
◆ ½ cup shelled pistachios

Sauté the rice in 1 tablespoon olive oil, stirring to coat thoroughly. (If substituting pistachio oil for the dressing, sauté the rice in sunflower oil instead of olive oil.) When the rice is transparent, add salt to taste and boiling water to cover, bring to a boil, and cover. Reduce the heat for 5 minutes and simmer, then turn off the heat and let the rice sit until it has absorbed all the water and is tender – about 25 minutes. (If necessary, add a drop or two of boiling water if the rice is still not tender. Stir, and leave for another 5 minutes.) Put the rice aside in a serving bowl to dry and cool.

In a small bowl, whisk together the lemon juice and the remaining olive oil (or pistachio oil). Season to taste, and add the lemon peel and pomegranate seeds. Set the mixture aside.

To the bowl with the rice add the parsley, scallions and pistachios. Stir in the lemon dressing. Cover and chill for at least 2 hours before serving.

SMALL ZUCCHINI PUFFS

AGGAH BI KOUSA

MAKES ABOUT 25–30 *AGGAHS*

Unlike the *aggah* above, this is less of an omelet and more of a *beignet*. It is light and a perfect accompaniment to drinks as well as a delightful *meze*.

- *6 small Zucchini, washed, trimmed and roughly chopped*
- *1 stick butter, cubed*
- *¾ cup water*
- *2 garlic cloves, finely chopped*
- *1 cup flour*
- *4 eggs*
- *3 tablespoons finely chopped parsley*
- *¼ teaspoon cayenne*
- *Salt and freshly ground pepper*
- *Oil for deep-frying*

Steam the zucchini in a steamer or saucepan with a little water. Remove from the heat when softened, and mash until smooth. Reserve.

Put the butter, water and garlic into a heavy saucepan. Bring to the boil.

Pour in the flour all at once, and stir with a wooden spoon or spatula until the batter leaves the sides of the saucepan. Scrape into a bowl and beat in the eggs, one at a time, until the batter is shiny. Beat in the mashed zucchini, together with the parsley, cayenne and seasoning to taste.

Heat the oil in a heavy saucepan or deep-fryer. Drop in the zucchini batter, teaspoonfuls at a time, and fry for about 5 minutes, until golden. Remove when done with a slotted spoon, and drain on paper towels. Keep the *beignets* warm while you finish frying the remaining batter. Serve warm with lemon wedges or Yogurt Sauce (page 108) for dipping.

CRACKED WHEAT AND HERB SALAD
TABBOULEH

SERVES 6

Probably the best-known of all Lebanese dishes outside the country, this salad has become a staple of summer parties and picnics in Britain, France and the United States, and is found in the display cabinet of every delicatessen. A true *tabbouleh,* however, customarily has more herbs to grain than is usually found in our Westernized versions.

- 1½ cups medium burghul
- 1 teaspoon salt
- Juice of 2 lemons
- 5 cups finely chopped flat-leaved parsley
- 3 cups finely chopped mint

- 2 tablespoons finely chopped scallion
- ¼ cup olive oil
- 3 plum tomatoes, seeded, drained and chopped
- ⅓ cucumber, seeded and finely chopped
- Salt and freshly ground pepper

In a large bowl, soak the burghul in salted boiling water (enough to cover) for 10 minutes, then rinse and drain thoroughly. Squeeze out any remaining moisture in a cloth or muslin. Transfer the burghul to another bowl, and add the juice of one lemon. Leave to soften for 1 hour.

To make the salad, combine the parsley, mint, scallion, oil, tomato and cucumber in a large bowl. Gently stir in the burghul, combining well. Season to taste and add more lemon juice, as desired. Chill slightly before serving.

LENTIL SALAD
SALAT 'AADS

SERVES 4–6

This salad is made with the earthy brown lentil beloved of peasants and farm workers. Despite the fact that they are considered the "food of the poor", lentils have an honored place in Lebanese cooking, and have made their way from the East and Middle East into European *cuisine bourgeoise.*

- 1¼ cups dried brown lentils, soaked for 1 hour
- 1 crushed red chili
- 1 teaspoon cumin seeds
- 1 bay leaf
- 5 tablespoons olive oil

- Juice of 1 lemon
- 2 garlic cloves, crushed
- Salt and freshly ground pepper
- 3 tablespoons finely chopped flat-leaved parsley

Drain the lentils and pick them over for debris. Rinse again and place in a saucepan of water to cover, together with the chili, cumin seeds and bay leaf. Bring to the boil, cover and simmer for about 30 minutes, or until tender. Drain thoroughly.

In a large bowl whisk together the oil, lemon juice, garlic and salt and pepper to taste. Add the warm lentils and the chopped parsley. Toss to combine, allow to cool, and chill for a couple of hours or overnight. (If there are leftovers, the lentils can be puréed or mashed, thinned with olive oil and more lemon juice, spiced with cayenne and fresh chopped coriander, and served as a dip).

SLICED CUCUMBER SALAD
SALAT KHIYAR

SERVES 6

Unlike the Arabic population of the Levant, the large Maronite and other Christian communities have no prohibition against alcohol. Wine, and here its derivative vinegar, feature in their recipes.

- *2 large cucumbers, peeled, halved, seeded and thinly sliced*
- *Salt and freshly ground pepper*
- *8 tablespoons finely chopped fresh mint*
- *4 tablespoons finely chopped flat-leaved parsley*
- *1 teaspoon orange blossom water or grated peel of ½ orange*
- *½ cup olive oil*
- *½ cup red wine vinegar*
- *5 tablespoons superfine sugar*

Place the cucumber slices in a strainer and toss liberally with salt. Leave to drain for 30 minutes.

In a large bowl put the parsley and orange water or peel. Whisk in the olive oil, red wine vinegar and the sugar until combined, and until the sugar has dissolved. Mix in the mint.

Dry the cucumber slices with paper towels, then add to the vinaigrette. Toss gently to combine. Chill for several hours or overnight before serving.

CHICK-PEA SALAD
SALAT HOUMUS

SERVES 6

This salad is delicious as a first course or as an accompaniment to kebabs or other lamb dishes.

- 6 tablespoons olive oil
- 1 garlic clove, crushed
- 1 large Spanish onion, thinly sliced
- 1 red bell pepper, cored, seeded and chopped
- 1 tablespoon dried thyme
- ½ teaspoon cumin seeds
- 3 tablespoons lemon juice
- 5 cups chick-peas, drained and rinsed
- Salt and freshly ground pepper
- 2 hard-boiled eggs, chopped
- Flat-leaved parsley

Heat the oil in a saucepan and sauté the garlic clove and onion over medium heat, until limp and lightly colored. After a minute or two add the red bell pepper, thyme and cumin seeds. Take off the heat and scrape the contents of the pan, including the oil, into a large bowl. Whisk in the lemon juice.

Stir the rinsed and drained chick-peas into the dressing, season to taste, and gently fold in the chopped egg. Turn the beans into a serving bowl and garnish with the flat-leaved parsley.

SWEET-AND-SOUR EGG PLANT
BAZINJAN RAHIB

SERVES 6

This is the popular egg plant in another guise – one often served at the *mezze* table. It lacks the smoky flavor of *moutabal,* relying on texture and flavor contrast for appeal.

- ◆ 2 medium egg plant, trimmed and cubed
- ◆ Salt
- ◆ 4 garlic cloves, crushed
- ◆ 2 large, mild yellow onions, chopped
- ◆ ½ cup olive oil
- ◆ 2 teaspoons ground cumin
- ◆ 1 teaspoon paprika
- ◆ 1 tablespoon light brown sugar
- ◆ 3 medium tomatoes, seeded and chopped
- ◆ Juice of 1 lemon
- ◆ 4 tablespoons finely chopped coriander

In a strainer toss the cubed egg plant with plenty of salt. Leave to drain for 30 minutes. Pat dry.

Line a large baking pan with foil. In a bowl combine the egg plant, garlic, chopped onions, olive oil, cumin, paprika and sugar. Toss together gently until the egg plant is thoroughly coated with the oil and spices. Spread the egg plant in the lined baking pan, and bake in a preheated oven at 400° for about 40 minutes, stirring twice as they cook.

Add the tomatoes to the pan, tossing to combine, and moisten with a little more oil, if necessary. Return to the oven for a further 15–20 minutes, until the egg plant and tomatoes are both very soft.

Turn the cooked vegetables into a large bowl. Add the lemon juice and chopped coriander, stir to mix thoroughly, and bring to room temperature or chill slightly before serving.

CUCUMBER AND YOGURT SALAD
CACIK

SERVES 6

Called *tzatziki* in Greece, this creamy, slightly bitter salad is popular all over the Middle East, though it retains its Turkish name.

- ◆ 1 cucumber, peeled, halved, seeded and diced
- ◆ Salt
- ◆ 2 garlic cloves, crushed
- ◆ 1½ cups Greek-style yogurt
- ◆ Freshly ground white pepper
- ◆ 4 tablespoons finely chopped fresh mint

Put the diced cucumber in a strainer, sprinkle liberally with salt and toss to coat. Leave to drain for 30 minutes. Meanwhile, in a bowl, combine the garlic, yogurt, pepper to taste and the mint. Chill the mixture to let the flavors mingle.

Dry the drained cucumber with paper towels and add to the yogurt dressing. Toss gently to mix and serve immediately.

PARSNIP AND DATE SALAD

SERVES 4–6

This is an unusual salad, making use of a peasant stand-by – parsnip – and that manna of the desert, the date. It makes an interesting complement to meat salads (like the one following) or kebabs.

- ◆ 6 medium parsnips, topped, tailed and peeled
- ◆ 24 plump medjul dates, pitted
- ◆ 4 teaspoons lemon juice
- ◆ 1 tablespoon light brown sugar
- ◆ ½ cup Greek-style yogurt

Finely grate the parsnip into a large bowl. Chop the dates roughly and add them to the bowl. In a small bowl whisk together the lemon juice, sugar and yogurt, until the sugar is dissolved.

Fold the dressing into the parsnips and dates. Chill slightly and serve.

BEEF AND BARLEY SALAD

SERVES 4–6

Beef is far less usual in Lebanese cooking than lamb, which thrives on the rugged foothills and dry coastal plains. But demand for beef in hotels and restaurants in towns has resulted in a successful marriage of Western tastes and local flavorings. Barley is an introduction from the Turkish and Aremenian traditions, the sumac from Syrian. This salad takes 2–3 days to make.

- ◆ ½ cup sumac seeds
- ◆ 4 tablespoons olive oil
- ◆ 2 tablespoons red wine vinegar
- ◆ 1½ pounds sirloin steak, 1-inch thick
- ◆ 2½ cups chicken stock
- ◆ 1 cup pearl barley, rinsed and drained
- ◆ 1 red onion, finely chopped
- ◆ ¾ cup slivered blanched almonds, toasted
- ◆ 2¾ cups seedless green grapes, halved
- ◆ ½ teaspoon coriander
- ◆ Salt and freshly ground pepper
- ◆ Watercress
- ◆ Cucumber slices and radishes
- ◆ Lemon quarters

Make sumac juice by soaking the seeds in 1½ cups boiling water for 20–30 minutes. Strain, discard the seeds and bottle.

In a bowl, whisk together the olive oil, vinegar and 2 tablespoons sumac juice (the remainder can be refrigerated or frozen for future use). Pour the marinade into a large plastic bag, add the sirloin, seal the bag, and shake to coat the beef. Put the bag into a bowl and chill the meat in the marinade overnight.

To cook the meat, grill on a barbecue or under a hot broiler for about 8–10 minutes on each side, basting with the marinade, until the meat is seared and just cooked on the outside but pink inside. Let the meat cool and chill, covered, several hours or overnight.

Meanwhile, make the barley. Bring the chicken stock to the boil, add the barley, cover and simmer until tender – about 30 minutes. Drain, cool and chill overnight.

To assemble the salad, slice the meat into thin strips. Reserve a few strips and put the remainder in the bowl. Add the barley, red onion, almonds, halved grapes and coriander. Moisten the salad with a little of the marinade, season with salt and pepper to taste, and arrange on a bed of watercress. Arrange the reserved beef strips on top and garnish with cucumber slices, radishes and lemon quarters.

Parsnip and date salad

MELON SALAD WITH CARDAMOM

SERVES 6

This can be made with orange or green/white melons, but is most flavorful made with juicy bright Charantais or cantaloupe melons. This can be served as a fruity accompaniment to the main course – particularly lamb dishes – or as a light dessert.

◆ ½ cup Greek-style yogurt
◆ ½ teaspoon ground cardamom
◆ 1½ teaspoons honey
◆ scant ½ cup lemon or lime juice

◆ 2 medium melons, peeled, seeded and cubed (or shaped into balls with a melon baller)

In a small bowl, whisk together the yogurt, cardamom, honey and juice until thoroughly mixed. Place the melon balls or cubes in a serving bowl, pour over the dressing and gently toss the salad to combine. Serve immediately.

GRAPEFRUIT AND AVOCADO COMPOTE

SERVES 6

Served with Satsuma Dressing or a lemony vinaigrette, this makes a delicious first course or accompaniment to a meat salad. An Israeli-style dish, it found favor in the hotel cuisine that once flourished in Beirut.

◆ 2 sweet pink grapefruit, peeled, pith removed, divided into segments
◆ 2 large ripe avocados, peeled and pitted, cut into cubes into cubes

◆ ½ cup Satsuma Dressing (page 112) or Classic Vinaigrette (page 107)
◆ 2 tablespoons blanched almond slices, toasted

In a serving bowl, combine the pink grapefruit and the avocado. Pour over the dressing and toss gently to combine. Scatter over the toasted almonds and serve immediately.

SWEET-AND-SOUR ZUCCHINI
KOUSA BE ZEIT

A relative of the egg plant, the zucchini has not quite attained the popularity of that vegetable in Lebanon. However, this cooked salad is one dish that finds appreciative appetites, either as a *mezze* or side dish. This Francophile version also uses wine vinegar as well as lemon juice, but the juice alone may be used to impart a more Arabian flavor.

- ½ cup olive oil
- 1 red onion, finely chopped
- 2 pounds zucchini, scrubbed trimmed and cut into thin 2-inch strips
- 2 tablespoons white wine vinegar
- 2 tablespoons lemon juice
- 2 tablespoons superfine sugar
- 1 teaspoon coriander seeds
- 1 teaspoon dill seeds
- ½ teaspoon cinnamon
- Salt and pepper
- 2 tablespoons pine nuts, toasted
- 2 tablespoons currants

Heat the oil in a skillet and sauté the onion gently for about 5 minutes, until softened but not colored. Stir in the zucchini and cook for a further 10 minutes, until also softened. Pour in the vinegar and lemon juice, and stir in the sugar, coriander and dill seeds, cinnamon and salt and pepper to taste. Simmer for about 5 minutes, then add the pine nuts and currants. Cook for a further 4–5 minutes, until the liquid has evaporated somewhat and the zucchini have become glazed.

Chill for several hours or overnight before serving.

BEETROOT SALAD
SALAT BANGAR

SERVES 4–6

This combination of a dairy product and beetroot has echoes of Russian and Polish cuisine, although those countries would use sour cream rather than yogurt. The addition of olive oil and cumin, however, is distinctly Levantine, while the optional ricotta – a type of which is made in the Lebanon – provides a richer texture.

- ◆ *2 tablespoons olive oil*
- ◆ *2 tablespoons lemon juice*
- ◆ *1 cup Greek-style yogurt*
- ◆ *½ teaspoon cumin seeds*
- ◆ *¼ cup ricotta cheese (optional)*
- ◆ *Salt and freshly ground pepper*
- ◆ *1 pound cooked beetroot, thinly sliced*
- ◆ *Chopped mint leaves*

In a large bowl, whisk together the oil and lemon juice with a fork. Stir in the yogurt and cumin seeds. With the back of the fork, mash in the ricotta, if used. Season the mixture to taste. Gently fold in the beetroot.

Transfer the salad to a serving bowl and garnish with chopped mint leaves. Chill or serve immediately.

FISH

SAMAK

CLAMS OR MUSSELLS TYRE STYLE

SERVES 4–6

Tyre was renowned in ancient times for its purple dye, reserved for Roman aristocrats and derived from the crushed shells of whelks. But that was not the only shellfish that thrived on the sea-shelf fronting the harbor. Mussels, several types of clam, shrimp and crayfish graced the Tyrean table and were transported inland. The tradition remains.

- 1 garlic clove, crushed
- 1 small red onion, thinly sliced
- 1 cup white wine
- 2 pounds clams or small mussels
- 4 plum tomatoes, peeled, seeded and chopped
- 2 tablespoons lemon juice
- 1 tablespoon semnah or butter
- 1 tablespoon finely chopped fresh coriander

Put the garlic and chopped onion with the wine in a deep saucepan. Bring to the boil, simmer for 2 minutes, then add the mussels or clams. Bring back to the boil, lower the heat and simmer, covered, for about 5 minutes, or until the shellfish open. Discard any mussels or clams that have not opened.

Remove the shellfish to a serving bowl and keep them warm. Add the tomatoes to the cooking liquid, and mash them into it. Bring it back to the boil and reduce slightly. Just before serving, stir in the lemon juice, *semnah* or butter, and the chopped coriander. Pour over the clams or mussels and serve immediately, with *khoubz* (Arab bread) or pita to mop up the sauce.

LEBANESE TUNA SALAD

SERVES 6–8

Although fresh tuna is available along the coast, canned tuna is just as popular as a convenience food as it is in the West. This version makes a delicious change from the more unusual Western tuna salads and can serve as a great filling for *khoubz* or pita bread.

- ◆ 3 medium-sized red bell peppers
- ◆ 2 garlic cloves, crushed
- ◆ Salt and freshly ground pepper
- ◆ 3 tablespoons lemon juice
- ◆ ½ cup olive oil
- ◆ 1 large red onion, finely chopped
- ◆ 2 tablespoons finely chopped fresh coriander
- ◆ ¾ cup pitted black olives, sliced
- ◆ 2 hard-boiled eggs, chopped
- ◆ 2 × 7-ounce can white tuna in oil or brine
- ◆ Lemon wedges

Place the 3 bell peppers on a rack under a hot pre-heated broiler, and cook, turning occasionally, until the skins are charred and blackened. Remove the bell peppers and place them in a paper or plastic bag and leave for 15 minutes.

Meanwhile, mash the garlic in a large bowl with a little salt until you have a paste. Whisk in the lemon juice and then the olive oil in a slow stream, until the dressing is emulsified. Stir in the onion and coriander.

Remove the bell peppers from the bag and skin them. Core and seed them, cut away the inner ribs, then cut the flesh into short thin strips. Stir the bell pepper strips into the dressing, cover and chill for 1 hour.

Gently fold in the olives, chopped eggs and flaked tuna. Stir to combine. Transfer the salad to a serving platter and garnish with lemon wedges.

PISTACHIO-FRIED FISH
SAMAK BI PISTACHIO

SERVES 6

In Lebanon, the white fish used for this dish might be grouper (*merou*) or sea bream (*farrideh*). Here sole or bass would do as well.

- ◆ ½ cup fine dry breadcrumbs
- ◆ 1 cup shelled pistachios, finely chopped and crushed
- ◆ 3 tablespoons finely chopped flat-leaved parsley
- ◆ Salt and freshly ground pepper
- ◆ 2 eggs
- ◆ 6 × 5-ounce white fish fillets
- ◆ ⅓ cup semnah or a combination of butter and olive oil
- ◆ Juice of 2 oranges
- ◆ Toasted chopped pistachios
- ◆ Orange wedges

On a large plate, mix together the breadcrumbs, crushed nuts, parsley and seasoning to taste. In a shallow bowl, beat the two eggs lightly.

Dip the fish pieces, one at a time, into the egg. Drain briefly, then coat both sides in the nut mixture, patting them to ensure an even covering. Shake off any excess mixture.

Heat half of the *semnah*, or half of the butter and oil mixture, in a large skillet. Sauté the fillets, 3 at a time, for about 5 minutes on each side, turning once with a spatula. Remove and keep warm while frying the remaining 3 fillets.

Before serving, deglaze the pan with the orange juice. Arrange the fillets on a serving platter, pour over the pan juices and serve, garnished with toasted pistachios and oranges wedges.

FISH AND RICE IN BROTH
SAYADIEH

SERVES 6

This is one of the most popular Arab fish dishes and a firm favorite of Lebanese fish restaurants. Each chef has his own particular twist – some sauté the fish first, some stew it; some purée the onions, some keep them whole; the garnishes vary as well. The following is a representative version.

- ◆ *1 cup flour*
- ◆ *Salt and freshly ground pepper*
- ◆ *Large pinch ground chili pepper*
- ◆ *6 × 5 ounces white fish fillets – sea bass, cod or halibut*
- ◆ *1 cup olive oil*
- ◆ *4 onions, chopped*
- ◆ *1 teaspoon ground cumin*
- ◆ *Juice of 2 lemons*
- ◆ *2⅓ cups long-grain rice*
- ◆ *2 tablespoons sliced blanched almonds, toasted*
- ◆ *Chopped flat-leaved parsley*

On a large plate mix together the flour, salt and pepper to taste, and a pinch of chili; toss with the hands to combine. Dip each of the fillets in the seasoned flour, shake off excess and put aside.

Heat 3 tablespoons of the oil in a large casserole with a cover, and sauté three of the fillets for about 8–10 minutes, until just opaque, turning once. Take the fish out, add a little more oil, and cook the remaining three fillets until done. Keep all the cooked fillets warm in a very low oven, covered with foil.

Add the remaining oil to the pan, stir in the chopped onions and sauté over medium-low heat, until they are softened and very lightly colored. Pour over 4–5 cups of water, bring to the boil, cover, and reduce the heat. Cook for about 10 minutes, until the onions are mushy. Pour the broth into a blender or food processor and purée in batches until it is smooth.

Return half the broth to the casserole, add salt to taste, the juice of 1 lemon and the rice. Add a little more water to cover, if necessary. Bring to the boil, cover and cook for a few minutes on high heat, then reduce the heat and cook for about 10 minutes over low heat. Take the rice off the heat, and allow to sit, covered, for another 10 minutes, until it is soft and fluffs with a fork.

Meanwhile put the remaining half of the onion broth in a small saucepan, add the remaining lemon juice and reduce the liquid over high heat to about half.

Transfer the rice to a heated serving dish with a rim, arranging it in a mound. Arrange the fillets around the rice, and pour over the lemon-onion broth. Sprinkle over the toasted almond slices and chopped parsley and serve immediately.

A Roman mosaic fish at Baalbek.

BARBECUED SARDINES

SERVES 4

Barbecued sardines are eaten in all the coastal ports of the Mediterranean, and Lebanon is no exception. The secret to their appeal is the freshness of the fish and the method of cooking – grilling over hot coals. If you do not have access to a barbecue, an oven broiler is an acceptable second best.

- ◆ *8 fresh small sardines, trimmed, cleaned, de-scaled*
- ◆ *scant ½ cup olive oil*
- ◆ *Juice of 1 lemon*
- ◆ *1 teaspoon ground cardamom*
- ◆ *2 tablespoons finely chopped flat-leaved parsley*
- ◆ *Salt and freshly ground pepper*
- ◆ *Lemon slices*

Wash the fish under running water, making sure all the scales have been removed. Wash the inside of the fish as well. Pat dry with paper towels.

In a bowl, mix together the oil, lemon juice, cardamom and chopped parsley. Spoon over the fish and rub in with the fingers. Season the dish to taste with salt and pepper.

Cook the fish on the barbecue or under a preheated hot broiler for about 3 minutes a side, basting with the flavored oil. Cook until the skin is charred and the flesh is white, and flakes easily with a fork.

Remove to a warmed platter and pour the remaining oil over the fish. Serve garnished with lemon slices.

CHILLED CUCUMBER AND MINT SQUID

SERVES 6

Like all Mediterranean cuisines, that of Lebanon makes good use of two of the stranger denizens of the deep – octopus and squid. This is a summery salad, which can be extended with other seafood if required.

◆ 3 pounds cleaned small
    squid, cut into rings
    and strips
◆ 1 cup fish stock
◆ 1 cup dry white wine
◆ 4 scallions, finely
    chopped
◆ 2 cucumbers, peeled,
    halved and seeded,
    and thinly sliced
◆ 18 cherry tomatoes,
    halved
◆ Lettuce leaves

DRESSING
◆ 1 tablespoon lemon juice
◆ 1 garlic clove, crushed
◆ ½ teaspoon superfine
    sugar
◆ 1 teaspoon Dijon
    mustard
◆ ½ cup olive oil
◆ Large pinch cayenne
    pepper
◆ ½ teaspoon ground
    cumin
◆ 1 tablespoon finely
    chopped mint leaves
◆ 1 cup Greek-style yogurt

In a large saucepan, combine the squid, fish stock and wine. Bring to the boil, cover and simmer for about 40 minutes or until tender, stirring occasionally to move the squid pieces around. Drain the squid and pat dry. Allow to cool.

Meanwhile make the dressing. In a large bowl, whisk together the lemon juice, garlic, sugar and mustard. Slowly add the oil in a stream, whisking, until the dressing is emulsified. Beat in the cayenne to taste, ground cumin and the mint leaves. Then gently stir in the yogurt, mixing it in thoroughly.

Add the cooled squid to the bowl and toss gently to coat in the yogurt dressing. Chill the squid for 2–3 hours. Before serving, gently fold in the chopped scallions, sliced cucumber and halved tomatoes, and arrange on a bed of lettuce.

FISH IN SESAME SAUCE
SAMAK BI TAHINI

SERVES 6

Tahini (sesame seed) paste can be bought at most delicatessens. The sauce made with *tahini* is often called simply *taratoor*, but should not be confused with the pine nut *Taratoor* (page 104). The sesame *taratoor* used in this recipe is usually baked with fish or cauliflower.

- *1²⁄₃ cups* taratoor bi tahini *(page 106)*
- *½ cup olive oil*
- *2 large onions, thinly sliced*
- *6 white fish fillets (brill, sea bass, or suchlike)*
- *Salt and freshly ground pepper*

Make the *taratoor* first, and set it aside.

Heat the olive oil in a skillet. Add the onions and sauté, stirring frequently, until they are limp and lightly golden.

Preheat the oven to 350°.

Transfer the onions to a large baking dish. Roll each of the fillets in the onions to coat with the oil, then arrange the fish on top of the onions, skin side up. Season to taste, cover with foil and bake for 15 minutes. Remove, and if desired, pass the fish under a hot broiler for a few minutes to crisp the skin.

Spoon the *taratoor* sauce over the fish and onions. Return the fish to the oven at the same temperature and bake, uncovered, for a further 20–25 minutes, or until the sauce is bubbling. Serve with pilau rice.

BAKED FISH
SAMAK FILFORN

SERVES 4–6

This common Western method of baking fish has been adopted by the Lebanese with enthusiasm, since it suits much of the typical Mediterranean catch, allows spices to be rubbed into the fish, and is admirably suited to fish that are to be served cold. The last of these is a popular Lebanese treatment, with the chilled, whole fish or fillets covered in *Taratoor bi Tahini* (page 106) or *Nougada* (page 95) sauce, or served with Green Mayonnaise (page 110) or Lemon Relish (page 111).

- *1 garlic clove, crushed*
- *Juice of ½ lemon*
- *½ cup olive oil*
- *2 teaspoons oregano*
- *Salt and freshly ground pepper*
- *1 whole sea bass, or 2–3 whole red mullet, depending on size*
- *Lemon wedges (optional)*

In a small bowl, mash the garlic into the lemon juice until you have a paste. Whisk in the olive oil, until emulsified, then the oregano and seasoning to taste.

Place the fish on a large piece of foil, and pour some of the marinade over it. Rub it into the fish on both sides. Close the foil over the fish, and chill for 1–2 hours.

Preheat the oven to 350°. Open the foil, pour over a little more marinade, and seal again. Place on a baking sheet and cook for 40–50 minutes, depending on the number and size of the fish. Test by inserting a knife or skewer into the flesh; it should be opaque.

Serve hot with lemon wedges, or cold – with the skin removed – embellished with one of the above-mentioned sauces or with the sauce served alongside.

BAKED STUFFED FISH
SAMAK HARRAH

SERVES 6

This is a recipe with many variations. The optional pomegranate seeds are an introduction from Iran, but one that is much appreciated in Lebanon. If the stuffed fish is white-fleshed, it is often served cold with a *Taratoor bi Sonoba* (Pine Nut Sauce); if an oily fish, it is always served hot, without sauce, simply garnished with lemon wedges.

◆ 4 pound sea bass or mullet, cleaned, gutted and scaled (or 10 ounce whole mackerel)
◆ Olive oil
◆ Salt and freshly ground pepper
◆ 1 small onion, finely chopped
◆ ½ green bell pepper, finely chopped
◆ ⅔ cup pine nuts
◆ ½ teaspoon bruised coriander seeds
◆ ½ cup fresh breadcrumbs
◆ 2–3 tablespoons white raisins

◆ 2 tablespoons pomegranate seeds (optional)
◆ 5 tablespoons finely chopped flat-leaved parsley
◆ 4 tablespoons fresh lemon juice
◆ Lemon wedges or Taratoor bi Sonoba (page 104; optional)
◆ Cucumber, olives, tomatoes, green bell peppers, pimento, anchovies, hard-boiled eggs, toasted pine nuts (optional)

If you are stuffing one whole white fish, rub it liberally with olive oil and rub in salt and pepper to taste. Leave to chill for 1 hour.

If using mackerel, do not buy the fish gutted; take them home whole. Sever the heads, leaving them attached by a small piece of skin. Snap the tail sharply, breaking the backbone inside the fish, and roll it back and forth to loosen the bone and flesh.

Using a spoon, scoop out the innards of the fish, and follow this by drawing out the loosened backbone. Use the spoon to press the flesh against the sides of the fish, enlarging the hole for stuffing. Wash the fish inside and out, pat dry and set aside.

To make the stuffing, heat 3 tablespoons olive oil. Sauté the onion for about 5 minutes over medium heat, stirring, until softened. Add the green bell pepper and continue stirring, until it is soft and the onions are changing color. Stir in the pine nuts for another 2 minutes, then the crushed coriander seeds and breadcrumbs. Stir for about 1 minute. Remove the pan from the heat and add the raisins, pomegranate seeds (if used) and the parsley. Season the stuffing with salt and pepper to taste, and moisten it with 1 tablespoon lemon juice.

Preheat the oven to 400°. Stuff the large white fish or the smaller mackerel with the mixture. Secure the white fish with a little thread or small skewers; fill the mackerel through the top opening and replace the heads as well as possible. Arrange the fish on a baking sheet, pour over the remaining lemon juice (and more oil on the white fish, if this is necessary).

Place the fish in the preheated oven and bake, covered loosely with foil, for about 40–45 minutes for the whole fish, or about 30 minutes for the six mackerel.

Remove from the oven. Serve the mackerel immediately with lemon wedges; the white fish may also be served hot or it may be allowed to cool and served with the *taratoor*.

In the latter case, the fish is usually garnished with paper-thin cucumber slices, olive rings, tomato roses with green bell pepper leaves, pimento and anchovy strips, hard-boiled egg slices and toasted pine nuts.

SARDINE-STUFFED LEMONS
HAMID MASHI WI SAERDIN

SERVES 6

Sardines, like lentils, are a traditional food of the poor, which now have considerable cachet among the foodies. Coastal Lebanon has always appreciated them, however, usually simply grilled (page 69) or stuffed and baked (see Baked Stuffed Fish, page 72). This is a different presentation, eaten as a light lunch or a European-style first course.

- ◆ *3 plump round lemons*
- ◆ *2 × 5-ounce can sardines packed in oil, drained*
- ◆ *3 tablespoons mayonnaise*
- ◆ *1½ tablespoons Dijon mustard*
- ◆ *1 large celery stick, finely chopped*
- ◆ *4 scallions, finely chopped*
- ◆ *2 tablespoons finely chopped flat-leaved parsley*
- ◆ *Salt and freshly ground pepper*
- ◆ *2 tablespoons pine nuts, toasted*
- ◆ *Green olives, cut lengthwise into slivers*

Halve the lemons and squeeze them with a juicer, reserve the juice. Take each half and carefully cut a thin slice from the bottom so that it will stand. With your fingers, try to remove as much as possible of the inner membrane from each half. Place the halves upside down for a few minutes.

Meanwhile place the drained sardines into a bowl. Mash together with the mayonnaise, mustard and 2 tablespoons of the lemon juice. Try to obtain a fairly smooth paste. Work in the chopped celery, onions and parsley. Season to taste and give a final stir.

Divide the sardine paste among the six lemon halves, shape the tops attractively and garnish with a few toasted pine nuts and slivers of green olive. Chill briefly (or up to 2 hours) and serve with warm *khoubz* (Arab bread) or pita.

FISH KEBABS
SAMAK KEBAB

SERVES 6

Kebabs are one of the most typical dishes of the Middle East. Those made with fish, however, are usually encountered only along the coast. Kebabs are usually cooked over hot coals, but these fish kebabs work well under a broiler. They go well with Lemon Relish (page 110).

- ◆ *4 onions, roughly chopped*
- ◆ *Juice of 3 lemons*
- ◆ *¼ cup olive oil*
- ◆ *Large pinch cayenne pepper*
- ◆ *2 teaspoons cumin*
- ◆ *1 tablespoon tomato paste*
- ◆ *2 bay leaves*

- ◆ *2 pound fillet of sea bass, cut into 1-inch cubes*
- ◆ *18–24 cherry tomatoes*
- ◆ *6 baby Zucchini, trimmed, scrubbed and cut into 3–4 pieces each*
- ◆ *Olive oil*
- ◆ *Lemon wedges*

Using a garlic press, squeeze the juice from the onion pieces a little at a time, until you have extracted as much as you can. In a bowl mix the onion juice with the lemon juice and whisk in the oil, cayenne to taste, cumin and tomato paste. Add the bay leaves.

Place the cubed fish in a larger bowl and pour the marinade over it; toss the fish using the hands. Cover and leave to chill for 1 hour.

On 6 large or 12 small skewers, thread the fish cubes, baby zucchini and cherry tomatoes. Place over hot coals or under a preheated hot broiler, and brush with a little oil, especially on the vegetables. Cook for about 10–15 minutes, turning once or twice, until the fish is opaque and the zucchini are just tender. Serve immediately with lemon wedges and rice or burghul.

POULTRY AND EGGS
TOUYOUR WI BEID

BARBECUED GARLIC CHICKEN
FARROUGE MISHWA

SERVES 4–6

This treatment is particularly good with whole poussins, split in half, flattened with a mallet and rubbed with paprika, then submerged in the marinade. It can also be made with tender chicken pieces.

- ◆ 3 x 1½-pound poussins, halved and flattened, or 6–8 chicken pieces
- ◆ 1 tablespoon paprika
- ◆ Salt and freshly ground pepper
- ◆ 4 tablespoons Taratoor bi Sade (page 111) or

- ◆ 3 garlic cloves, crushed
- ◆ 3 tablespoons olive oil
- ◆ 2–4 tablespoons lemon juice
- ◆ Fresh watercress
- ◆ Lemon quarters

Rub the flattened chicken halves or pieces with the paprika and salt and pepper, making sure that the spices are well distributed. In a small bowl, whisk together the *taratoor*, olive oil and 2 tablespoons lemon juice. (Alternatively, if no *taratoor* is available, mash the garlic with the oil, then whisk in 4 tablespoons lemon juice.)

Pour the marinade over the chicken, turning the pieces in it. If necessary, add a little more oil. Cover and chill overnight.

Barbecue the poussin halves or chicken pieces over hot coals, which are whitening with ash. Turn 3 or 4 times, until browned and lightly charred on the outside, but succulent within. This will take 20–40 minutes, depending on the size of the pieces. Check by inserting a skewer into a meaty part; the juice should run clear. (Alternatively, cook under a preheated broiler, turning occasionally, until done.)

Serve the chicken hot, on a bed of watercress with lemon quarters for squeezing over.

GARLIC CHICKEN WINGS
JAWANEH

SERVES 6

The method of marinating and cooking these wings is very like *Farrouge Mishwa* (page 76). However, chicken wings are a particular favorite of the Lebanese, often served as a *meze*, and therefore deserve a name of their own.

- ◆ *12–18 chicken wings, tips trimmed off*
- ◆ *2 teaspoons paprika*
- ◆ *1 teaspoon ground cumin*
- ◆ *3–4 garlic cloves, crushed*
- ◆ *Salt and freshly ground pepper*
- ◆ *Juice of 1 lemon*
- ◆ *4–5 tablespoons olive oil*
- ◆ *½ cup Taratoor bi Tahini (page 106)*

Wash the chicken wings and pat dry. Rub in the paprika and cumin with your hands. In a small bowl, mash the garlic cloves with salt and pepper to taste, then whisk in the lemon juice and oil until combined. Pour over the chicken wings in a shallow dish, turning to coat them.

Cook the wings for about 20 minutes over hot coals, which have turned grey, turning and basting the wings with the marinade until they are tender, but cooked inside and golden brown and slightly charred outside. (Alternatively, cook under a medium-hot preheated broiler, turning occasionally, until done.)

Spoon a little *taratoor bi tahini* in a strip down each wing and serve piping hot.

LEBANESE STUFFED CHICKEN
DAJAJ MASHI

SERVES 6

Stuffed poultry is a favorite all over the Arab world, from Morocco – where stuffing made with couscous, cinnamon and pickled lemon pieces – to Lebanon and Syria, where the staple ingredient varies between burghul and rice, both of which are usually enriched with nuts and herbs.

- *4 tablespoons semnah or butter*
- *8 ounces ground lamb*
- *1 large onion, finely chopped*
- *2 tablespoons pine nuts*
- *1 tablespoon raisins*
- *1⅓ cups long-grain rice*
- *Salt and freshly ground black pepper*
- *1 tablespoon honey*
- *3 tablespoons Greek-style yogurt*
- *4½ pound free-range roasting chicken*

Heat 1 tablespoon butter in a skillet. Gently sauté the ground lamb, stirring to ensure it browns all over. Transfer the meat with a slotted spoon to a plate, add another 1 tablespoon butter to the pan and stir in the finely chopped onion. Sauté over medium-low heat for about 5 minutes, until it is limp; add the pine nuts and continue to sauté until both onions and nuts are lightly colored. Add the raisins and rice, and stir for a minute or two until the rice is transparent; season to taste. Pour in 2 cups water and bring to the boil. Reduce the heat, cover and simmer for about 25 minutes, or until the rice has absorbed all the water. Leave until it is cool enough to handle.

Preheat the oven to 400°. Melt the remaining *semnah* or butter in a saucepan, take off the heat; stir in the honey until it melts, then the yogurt. Stuff the chicken with the rice mixture, and secure the opening with skewers. Leave the remaining rice in the pan to be warmed up later. Place the chicken in a roasting pan and baste generously with the yogurt sauce.

Roast for 20 minutes at the above temperature, then reduce the heat to 350°F for a further 1¼–1½ hours. Baste twice with the yogurt sauce. Test to see if the chicken is cooked by piercing the joint between body and thigh with a skewer; the juice should run clear.

Heat the remaining rice gently over low heat and moistened with a little of the chicken pan juices. Serve with the hot stuffed chicken.

Lemons flourish in the Lebanese climate.

CHICKEN WITH APRICOTS AND OLIVES

SERVES 8

This savory combination owes more to the Israeli taste than to classic Lebanese cuisine. Israel is Europe's richest source of dried fruits, and they make a frequent appearance in the meat stews and desserts of that country. However, taste cannot be confined by national borders, and dishes like this one have become common in Lebanon, adapted to include specialities such as *arak*.

- ◆ *3½ pounds skinned, boned and cubed chicken*
- ◆ *5 garlic cloves, crushed*
- ◆ *¾ cup chopped ready-to-eat dried apricots*
- ◆ *½ cup black Greek olives*
- ◆ *½ teaspoon grated orange peel*
- ◆ *5 tablespoons orange juice*

- ◆ *2 tablespoons lemon juice or white wine vinegar*
- ◆ *½ cup arak (anise-based Lebanese liqueur) or ouzo*
- ◆ *2 tablespoons fresh fennel leaves*
- ◆ *1½ tablespoons olive oil*
- ◆ *¾ cup light brown sugar*

Preheat the oven to 400°.

Combine all the ingredients except the sugar in a large bowl and stir carefully to mix well. Cover and chill overnight.

Transfer the chicken pieces to a baking pan and pour over the marinade, including the olives and apricots. Sprinkle over the sugar. Bake for about 30 minutes, turning once or twice.

Remove the chicken pieces to a serving platter, and arrange the olives and apricots over and around them. Strain the cooking juices into a saucepan, and reduce over high heat to about half. Pour the sauce over the chicken. Serve warm or cold.

MUSCAT BAKED ALMOND CHICKEN

SERVES 6

This dish is made with the sweet white-green grapes that have been grown around Cyprus and the Levant since Crusader times. Both a wine-making and a dessert grape, the muscat gives a pungent flavor and aroma to this recipe, which has its roots in a centuries-old tradition of using ground almonds as a thickening agent. In Lebanon, the herbs used would be wild – the marjoram, in particular, of a type found only in the eastern Mediterranean.

- 4½ pound free-range chicken
- Salt and freshly ground pepper
- ½ teaspoon cinnamon
- Large pinch nutmeg
- Fresh lemon thyme
- Fresh marjoram
- 3 cups muscat grapes, peeled, seeded and halved
- 1 cup sweet muscat wine
- 1 tablespoon semnah *or* butter
- 3 tablespoons sliced blanched almonds
- ½ cup ground almonds
- ½ cup light cream
- 2 egg yolks

Wash and pat dry the chicken, rub it all over with salt and pepper to taste, the cinnamon and the nutmeg.

Take 2–3 sprigs of lemon thyme and the same of marjoram and put them inside the chicken. Place it in a casserole, stuff with half the grapes and pour over the wine. Cover and cook the chicken in a preheated oven at 400° for 1½ hours.

Remove the chicken from the oven and transfer it to a warm serving platter. Remove the grapes and herbs from the cavity, joint the chicken and cover it with foil to keep it warm.

In a small saucepan, melt the *semnah* or butter and sauté the sliced almonds for a few minutes until just colored. Remove with a slotted spoon and set aside. Skim the fat from the chicken cooking juices in the casserole and strain them into the saucepan. Heat the juices gently until very hot, but not boiling, and stir in the remaining grapes and the ground almonds. Allow to cook for a few minutes to combine.

In a small bowl beat the cream and egg yolks together lightly. Take a spoonful of the hot chicken stock and stir it into the egg. Remove the saucepan from the heat and stir in the egg mixture; the sauce should thicken as your stir.

Pour some of the sauce over the jointed chicken and sprinkle it with the toasted almonds. Pour the remainder into a sauceboat to be served with *Mudardara* (page 98) or pilau rice.

CHEESE-FRIED EGGS
BEID BI GEBNA

SERVES 4

This dish is simplicity itself and combines two favorite Lebanese fried foods: eggs and cheese. The cheeses most usually used in Lebanon are versions of Kaseri or Halloumi; both are available from Greek, Turkish and Lebanese delicatessens in the West. Italian *pecorino* or one of the new hard English goat or ewe cheeses would make an authentically strong-tasting substitute.

- ½ teaspoon salt
- ½ teaspoon ground cumin
- 2 tablespoons semnah
- *or butter*
- 4 thick slices hard cheese
- 4 eggs

In a small salt-cellar or egg cup, mix together the salt and cumin. Reserve.

Heat the *semnah* or butter over medium heat. Add the four cheese slices and fry for about 3 minutes, or until they begin to bubble. Crack an egg over each slice, cover and cook gently, until the egg is just done. Lift the eggy cheeses out with a spatula and serve. Offer the cumin salt; take a pinch and sprinkle over the egg before eating.

ONION-FLAVORED HARD-BOILED EGGS
BEID HAMID

SERVES 6

These hard-boiled eggs are a Middle-Eastern favorite, with a quite distinctive flavor and a beige-brown color when peeled. They are a delicious foil to stews, such as *Bamia* (page 91), are occasionally served quartered as *mezze*, and make a fine snack with a salad, such as *Bazinjan Rahib* (page 59).

◆ *6 eggs*
◆ *Skins from 6 onions (reserve the onions for another use)*

◆ *Seasoned salt and/or lemon pepper (can be bought prepared in certain stores and delicatessens)*

Place the eggs in a saucepan and cover with the onion skins. Pour in enough cold water to cover and turn the heat as low as possible. Simmer very gently for about 6–7 hours, topping up the water when necessary. (Putting a layer of oil over the water will retard evaporation, but it must still be checked occasionally.)

When the time is up, plunge the eggs into cold water and leave to cool before peeling. Serve with the seasoned salt and/or pepper, as desired. The eggs can be kept refrigerated for up to 2 days without losing their flavor.

BRAISED DUCK WITH SWEET POTATOES

SERVES 6

Live ducks as well as chickens are common denizens of Lebanese street markets, and in smaller towns such feathered livestock will be found wandering the back roads around peasant houses. The sweet potato is an introduction from Central Africa, which has been accepted into the regional cuisine and into this Maronite recipe.

◆ *6 duck quarters, washed and patted dry*
◆ *Salt and freshly ground pepper*
◆ *2 carrots, chopped*
◆ *2 celery sticks, chopped*
◆ *1 large onion, chopped*
◆ *1 garlic clove, crushed*
◆ *1 bay leaf*
◆ *1 teaspoon thyme*
◆ *6 cardamom pods*
◆ *1 tablespoon tomato paste*

◆ *2 cups duck or chicken consommé*
◆ *4 medium sweet potatoes, peeled and roughly cubed*
◆ *1 tablespoon olive oil*
◆ *2 tablespoons superfine sugar*
◆ *4 tablespoons red wine vinegar*
◆ *1 tablespoon honey*
◆ *2 tablespoons white raisins*

Trim the duck of all extra skin and fat. Place the trimmings in a large shallow casserole, together with the duck quarters, seasoned with salt and pepper, and fry for about 20 minutes, until the trimmings are frizzled and the duck quarters are crisp and brown. Discard the trimmings, reserve the duck quarters, and strain the fat into a heavy saucepan.

Sauté the carrots, celery and onion in the saucepan for about 8 minutes, stirring until they are colored and the onion is limp. Pour off the fat, stir in the garlic briefly over the heat, and add the bay leaf, thyme, cardamom, tomato paste, consommé and 1 cup water. Stir to combine, bring to the boil, lower the heat slightly and simmer for 30 minutes, skimming once or twice.

Preheat the oven to 350°.

Place the duck back in the casserole, strain over the stock, cover and cook for about 40 minutes, or until the duck is done.

Meanwhile, put the sweet potatoes into the saucepan. Cover with water and bring to the boil. Cook for 5 minutes, then drain thoroughly. Reserve.

When the duck is cooked, remove the pieces from the casserole with a slotted spoon and strain off the juice into a bowl or fat separator. Add the olive oil to the casserole and sauté the drained sweet potatoes, stirring gently to coat all the sides, for about 5 minutes. Add the duck quarters and remove from the heat.

Skim the fat from the reserved duck stock. In a saucepan, cook the sugar and vinegar together, stirring until the mixture is beginning to caramelize. Whisk in the duck stock and honey until smooth.

Pour the sweet-sour sauce over the sweet potatoes and duck quarters, add the raisins, and cover the casserole. Simmer for about 10 minutes. Serve immediately from the casserole.

SOUR ORANGE TURKEY
HABISH WI LAEMON

SERVES 8

The turkeys that roam unfettered in the Levant are a small black-necked breed, tasty but not always tender. This sour marinade tenderizes the meat while lending a tangy fruitiness. Sour oranges were brought to southern Europe by the Arabs, where they became better known as "Seville oranges".

- ◆ *10–12 pound turkey*
- ◆ *6 sour (Seville) oranges*
- ◆ *4 garlic cloves, cut into slivers*
- ◆ *3 red or mild yellow onions*
- ◆ *2 tablespoons fresh marjoram, finely chopped*
- ◆ *¼ cup olive oil*
- ◆ *1 teaspoon ground coriander*
- ◆ *Salt and freshly ground pepper*
- ◆ *Flat-leaved parsley*
- ◆ *½ cup Greek-style yogurt (optional)*

Wash the turkey and pat it dry with paper towels. Squeeze the juice from 4 oranges; reserve the other 2 for the moment.

Make small gashes through the turkey skin into the flesh, and insert the garlic slivers into them. Slice two of the onions thinly into a large enamel-lined casserole, and place the turkey on top. Scatter the marjoram on top, and pour over the orange juice. Cover the bowl and chill for 1 day, turning the turkey several times in the marinade.

Preheat the oven to 400°.

Take the turkey from the marinade and pat it dry. Rub all over with the olive oil, ground coriander, and salt and pepper to taste. Remove the sliced onions from the marinade with a slotted spoon and arrange them over the bottom of a baking pan. Place the turkey on top, breast side down, and pour over the marinade. Roast in the oven for 10 minutes, then lower the heat to 325°, and continue roasting, basting with the pan juices occasionally, for a further 2½ hours, or until the juices run clear when the turkey is pierced with a skewer or sharp knife. If necessary, add some water to the liquid to keep it from drying out.

Remove the bird from the oven, place on a serving platter, and let it rest, covered, for 15 minutes. Strain the pan juices into a saucepan. Peel the two remaining oranges, separate them into segments, and add to the saucepan. Reduce the sauce over high heat until it thickens slightly. Cut the turkey meat into serving pieces, slice the breast and arrange on the serving platter. Slice the last onion and arrange the rings over the turkey pieces. Strain over the reduced juices and orange segments. Garnish with flat-leaved parsley and serve immediately.

The turkey may also be served cold with yogurt. Whisk some of the reduced juices and finely-chopped parsley into the yogurt before chilling it.

MEAT-BASED MAIN COURSES
AL-LAHEM

LEBANESE SHISH KEBAB
LAHEM MESHWI

SERVES 6

"Shish kebab" probably originated in Turkey, but its popularity has carried the skewered meat, in various forms, as far east as Thailand, as far west as the United States and as far north as Russia. The Levantine version is made with mutton or lamb; beef or liver can be substituted by the less orthodox. The vinaigrette-like marinade is an essential.

- 2 pounds tender lamb, leg or tenderloin, cut into 2-inch cubes
- 1 large onion, quartered
- 1 large sweet green bell pepper, cored and seeded
- 18 cherry tomatoes, stems removed

MARINADE
- 1 onion, finely sliced
- 2 tablespoons olive oil
- 3 tablespoons fresh lemon juice
- Salt and freshly ground pepper
- 1 teaspoon Taratoor bi Sade or 2 garlic cloves, crushed
- 1 dried red pepper, crushed (optional)
- 1 teaspoon ground cumin
- ½ teaspoon ground cinnamon
- Lemon quarters

Make the marinade first. Place the finely sliced onion in a large bowl. In a screw-top bottle, put together the other marinade ingredients except the lemon quarters (be more generous with the salt than you might normally be), cover and shake it vigorously to combine.

Put the lamb cubes (or other chosen meat) into the bowl, and pour over the marinade. Use your hands to toss the meat and marinade, so that everything is coated and well mixed. Cover the bowl and chill for at least 8 hours or as long as 24.

Cut each onion quarter in half and separate each of the 8 onion sections into 3 parts, so that you have 24 onion sections. Cut the green bell pepper into 18 squareish pieces. Remove the meat from the refrigerator.

Thread the bell pepper, meat, onion and tomatoes onto 6 large skewers, alternating the ingredients, but beginning and ending each skewer with green bell pepper.

Over grey-ashed charcoal, barbecue the kebabs for about 12–15 minutes, basting with the marinade and turning two or three times, until they are browned on the outside, but pink within. (Alternatively, cook on a rack under a preheated broiler, with a tray to catch the juices.) Serve the kebabs with rice and garnish generously with lemon quarters.

ARMENIAN BAKED GROUND MEAT
KOFTA BI SAYNIYEH

SERVES 6–8

Variations of these ground lamb "sausages" are encountered in the northeastern regions, influenced by Armenian and Syrian peoples, and are also popular among Lebanese immigrants in the United States and Europe. Shaped into small balls, they can be coated in flour and deep-fried; in this recipe they are baked in tomato sauce.

- *1 pound potatoes, peeled and quartered*
- *1 onion, chopped*
- *1½ pounds ground lamb or beef*
- *2 eggs*
- *4 tablespoons chopped parsley*
- *5 teaspoons fried mint*
- *1 teaspoon ground allspice*
- *Salt and freshly ground pepper*
- *5 tablespoons pine nuts*
- *5 tablespoons samneh or butter*
- *2 tablespoons tomato paste*
- *Red and yellow sweet bell pepper rings*
- *Lemon wedges*

Boil the potatoes until tender and then drain thoroughly. Put them into the bowl of a food processor fitted with a metal blade, together with the onion, and process until puréed. Add the ground meat, and process until the mixture is combined and of a paste-like consistency; add the eggs, herbs and spices, and season to taste. Process until all is combined, stopping the machine to scrape down the sides of the bowl once or twice. Chill the mixture for 1 hour.

Sauté the pine nuts in 2 tablespoons butter over medium heat until they are golden; cool slightly. Take the meat from the refrigerator and divide it into 8 balls. Place a sheet of greaseproof paper on a flat kitchen surface or a board, and flatten a ball into a longish rectangle. Place about ¾ tablespoon pine nuts down the center of the rectangle, and roll the meat into a cylinder or "sausage" around it, sealing the ends. Repeat with the remaining meatballs and pine nuts.

Preheat the oven to 350°.

Place the 8 sausages close together on an oiled baking sheet. In a small saucepan, melt the remaining *samneh* or butter and stir in the tomato paste, beating until combined. Pour the tomato butter over the meat, making sure to cover as much of the meat as possible. Bake for about 45–50 minutes, or until the *kofas* are browned and the sauce baked in.

Served garnished with red and yellow bell pepper rings and lemon wedges.

TRAY KIBBEH
KIBBEH BI SAYNIYEH

Although individual *kibbeh* (page 43) are more commonly served as *mezze*, this tray *kibbeh* can also be divided into small squares for hors-d'oeuvres. But it makes a delicious main course, its somewhat dry consistency well-complemented by *Bazinjan Rahib* (page 59), served at room temperature.

- ½ cup water
- ½ cup canned tomato juice
- ¼ cup fresh lemon juice
- 2½ cups fine-ground burghul
- 1 pound ground lamb
- 1 teaspoon paprika
- ½ teaspoon ground cumin
- Large pinch cayenne
- Salt and freshly ground pepper
- 1½ tablespoons sesame seeds (optional)
- ¼ cup melted samneh or butter
- 2 tablespoons sunflower oil

FILLING

- 1 tablespoon olive oil
- 1 onion, finely chopped
- 12 ounces ground lamb
- ½ cup chopped walnuts or pine nuts
- ½ teaspoon allspice
- Salt and freshly ground pepper

Make the *kibbeh* "pastry". In a bowl, stir together the water, tomato juice and lemon juice. Add the burghul, mix in and allow to rest for 10 minutes.

In the bowl of a food processor, combine the ground lamb, spices and salt and pepper to taste; process until the meat has been ground into a more paste-like consistency. Add the burghul and juice with the processor on, little by little, until it is combined thoroughly.

Remove the meat paste to a bowl and squeeze with the hands until it has a more elastic feel, then chill for 2 hours.

Meanwhile make the filling. In a skillet, heat the olive oil, and sauté the onion in it until it is limp and lightly colored. Add the ground lamb and cook, stirring, until the meat is browned. Take off the heat, drain off the excess fat and stir in the nuts, allspice and seasoning to taste.

Mix together the melted *semneh* or butter and the sunflower oil. Brush a little over the bottom of a square baking pan. Divide the chilled *kibbeh* "pastry" in half. Take small handfuls from one half and flatten between moistened hands. Press the pieces into the base of the pan, joining them up to form a bottom crust. Spoon in the filling, spreading it evenly over the *kibbeh*. Take more small handfuls from the second half of the *kibbeh* and make the top crust to go over the filling. Pat it on evenly up to the edges of the pan. Pat the sesame seeds, if used, into the crust.

Preheat the oven to 400°.

Divide the "pie" into serving pieces with a sharp knife – either large squares for a main course or small diamonds for a *mezze*. Brush with the *samneh* and oil mixture, allowing it to sink into the divisions. Bake the tray *kibbeh* for 10 minutes, then lower the heat to 350°, and bake for a further 30–35 minutes. Remove from the oven and allow to cool slightly before lifting the slices. Serve with Yogurt and Cucumber Sauce (page 108), if desired.

The tray *kibbeh* can also be chilled and served cold.

Flowers growing above lake Qaraoun.

LIVER WITH MINT
KIBDEH BI NA'NA

SERVES 4

This is an unusual combination of flavors to Western tastes, but is exquisite. If fresh mint is not available, half the quantity of dried mint can be used, although the result will not be as subtle – or as visually attractive.

- 4 *tablespoons* samneh *or combination of butter and olive oil*
- 1 *onion, finely sliced*
- 1 *garlic clove, crushed*
- 1 *pound calves' or lambs' liver, very thinly sliced*
- *Flour for dredging*
- *½ cups red wine vinegar*
- 2 *tablespoons very finely chopped fresh mint*

Heat 2 tablespoons *samneh* or the butter and oil over medium-high heat. Sauté the onion until it is limp, add the garlic and continue cooking until the onion is lightly colored. Remove the onion and garlic with a slotted spoon and reserve.

Quickly dredge the liver in the flour and shake off the excess. Add the remaining *samneh* or butter/oil to the pan and sauté the liver slices quickly on both sides. Return the onions and garlic to the pan, pour in the vinegar, and stir in the mint. Cook for about 5 minutes, spooning the sauce over the liver, until the liquid is reduced and glazes the meat.

LAMB KNUCKLE STEW
LAHMA BI HOUMUS WI TOMATIM

SERVES 4

Lamb knuckle is familiar to Western foodies as the main ingredient of that Greek taverna staple Lamb Kleftiko. It is an economical dish in any guise; in Lebanon it is often stewed with green beans, or as here, with chick-peas.

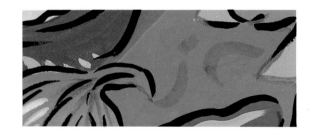

- 1 tablespoon olive oil
- 2 onions, sliced
- 3 garlic cloves, finely chopped
- 1 teaspoon allspice
- 2 teaspoons ground cumin
- Pinch crushed dried red pepper flakes
- 1 bay leaf, crushed
- 4 meaty knuckles of lamb (about 12 ounces each)
- 2 x 14-ounce cans chick-peas, drained and rinsed
- 2 x 14-ounce cans chopped tomatoes
- 2 cups lamb or beef stock
- Salt and freshly ground pepper
- 1 lemon
- 1 cup chopped coriander

  coriander

Preheat the oven to 475°.

Pour the oil into a casserole in which the knuckles will fit in one layer with space to spare. Heat over medium heat, add the sliced onion and sauté for 4 minutes, then add the garlic and continue cooking until the onion and garlic are limp and lightly colored, about 6 minutes.

Remove the hot onions with a slotted spoon to a large bowl, stir in the spices and bay leaf, and reserve. Add the knuckles to the casserole, turning in the oil to brown them. Transfer the casseroled lamb to the oven, and bake for 35 minutes, turning the knuckles occasionally.

Add the chick-peas, tomatoes and stock to the onions in the bowl and mix together. Remove the casserole from the oven, pour the chick-pea and tomato mixture over the knuckles and season to taste. Bring the stew to the boil on top of the stove, then cover and continue baking for another hour on the lower shelf of the oven. Test the knuckle with a knife for doneness; it should pierce easily.

Squeeze over the juice from the lemon and sprinkle the coriander over the stew. Serve immediately.

STEWED MEAT AND OKRA
BAMIA MASLU

For a change, this dish is usually made with beef, although lamb may also be used. The okra does not have to be parboiled, but if it is not it has a rather glutinous consistency – a trait not despised by the Lebanese, but generally rather disliked in the West. The choice is yours.

- *2 pounds okra (ladies' fingers)*
- *4 tablespoons* samneh *or combination of butter and olive oil*
- *2 onions, finely sliced*
- *1 garlic clove, crushed*
- *1½ pounds lean braising beef, cut into 1-inch cubes*
- *3 tablespoons tomato paste*
- *1½ cups hot beef stock*
- *Salt and freshly ground pepper*
- *2 tablespoons red wine vinegar or lemon juice*
- *2 tablespoons finely chopped coriander*

Trim the stems off the okra. (If you are very careful, and manage to trim the stems without cutting into the inner ribbed section of the okra, it will not bleed on cooking, and you can avoid parboiling.) Bring a large saucepan of water to the boil. Drop in the trimmed okra, bring back to the boil, and cook for 3 minutes. Drain thoroughly.

Heat 3 tablespoons of the *samneh* or butter and oil in a heatproof casserole, and sauté the onion over medium heat for 5 minutes, or until limp. Add the garlic and continue to cook for another few minutes, until the onion is lightly colored. Remove the onion with a slotted spoon and add the last 1 tablespoon *samneh* and the meat. Sauté, turning and stirring, until the meat is browned all over. Add the drained okra and fry for about 3 more minutes, then return the onions to the casserole.

Stir the tomato paste into the heated beef stock, season, and pour the liquid over the meat and vegetables. Bring back to the boil, cover and lower the heat. Simmer, stirring occasionally, for about 1 hour 45 minutes, or until the meat is very tender when pierced. Top up the liquid with a little water during cooking, if necessary. Just before serving, stir in the red wine vinegar or lemon juice and the chopped coriander. Serve immediately.

STUFFED COURGETTES
KOUSA MASHI

SERVES 4

This dish is usually made with ground lamb, but it can be varied with beef. For the vegetable, egg plant or any small squash can be used. The Lebanese and Syrians use a special vegetable corer, called a *munara*, to make this dish. An apple corer, knife or a small melon baller will do as well.

- 2 tablespoons olive oil
- 1 onion, finely chopped
- 1 garlic clove, finely chopped
- ⅓ cup raisins
- ⅔ cup uncooked long-grain rice
- 1 teaspoon dried mint
- 1 teaspoon Lebanese spice (page 16)
- 4 medium-sized zucchini
- (about 7 inches long and ½-inch diameter)
- 8 ounces ground lean lamb
- Salt and freshly ground pepper
- 2½ cups lamb or beef stock
- Fresh mint leaves
- Fresh yellow zucchini blossoms (optional)

Heat the olive oil in a saucepan. Sauté the onion for 6 minutes, until limp, then add the garlic and continue cooking until they are both lightly colored. Remove from the heat and stir in the raisins, rice, mint and spice. Allow to cool slightly.

Meanwhile, core the zucchini. Cut off the stem ends and carefully hollow out each zucchini, leaving a thin ⅛-inch shell. Set aside.

Scrape the rice mixture into the bowl of a food processor fitted with a metal blade. Process very briefly to chop the ingredients coarsely. Return to the saucepan or a bowl. Put the ground lamb into the processor and run the machine, pulsing and stopping to scrape down the sides, until the meat is a fine paste. Add the meat to the rice mixture and knead the two together until smooth.

Using your fingers and a long-handled spoon, carefully stuff each zucchini with some of the meat mixture, filling it as tightly as possible.

Pour the stock into a shallow casserole or heatproof baking pan with a cover. Add the zucchini, season to taste, and cover. Bring to the boil, then lower the heat and simmer for about 25 minutes, or until the zucchini are tender.

Transfer the zucchini to a serving platter, and garnish with fresh mint leaves and zucchini blossoms, if available. Serve the stuffed zucchini with the reduced stock or with Yogurt and Cucumber Sauce (page 108).

A vineyard in the Bekkah valley.

LAMB KEBABS
KOFTA HALAKUYEH

SERVES 6–8

Variations of ground "rolls" are found all over the Middle East, Greece, Turkey and the Balkan states, and are well-known in the West from their frequent appearance on "kebab house" menus. What distinguishes the national versions are the spicing and special ingredients and, as in the Armenian *Kofta* (page 87), the method of cooking. This Lebanese recipe is satisfying but simple.

- ◆ *4 slices bread, crusts removed and cubed (about 3 cups)*
- ◆ *1 garlic clove, crushed*
- ◆ *2 pounds ground lamb*
- ◆ *2 small onions, grated*
- ◆ *¼ cup ground cumin*
- ◆ *½ teaspoon cayenne*
- ◆ *3 tablespoons finely chopped parsley*
- ◆ *1 egg*
- ◆ *Salt and freshly ground pepper*
- ◆ *Lemon wedges*

Place the bread cubes in a small bowl and add enough water to dampen them – about 4–5 tablespoons. Add the garlic and, with the hands, mash the bread and garlic with the water. Leave to stand for about 10 minutes.

In a large bowl, mix together the ground lamb, grated onion, cumin, cayenne and parsley. Work with the hands to combine. Knead in the bread paste, the egg and seasoning to taste, until everything is mixed and the meat has absorbed the liquid and become drier and smoother.

With the hands, roll the meat into 6–8, long cylinders. Pass a skewer through each cylinder and pat the meat around to secure it.

Cook the kebabs over grey-ashed coals for about 20 minutes, until they are brown on all sides. (Alternatively, cook under a hot broiler, turning two or three times, until done.)

Serve the kebabs with the lemon wedges and with *Caçik* (page 59), if desired.

SPICED LAMB CHOPS
KASTALETA GHANAM

SERVES 6

These spiced chops bear more than a passing resemblance to the lamb tandoori dishes of India, and show how influences have passed from one part of the Muslim world to another.

- *½ cup* samneh *or butter*
- *½ teaspoon* Lebanese *spice (page 16)*
- *¼ teaspoon ground cardamom*
- *¾ teaspoon ground ginger*
- *¼ teaspoon ground nutmeg*
- *Large pinch of coriander*
- *Pinch of cloves*
- *1 tablespoon freshly chopped mint*
- *1 tablespoon freshly chopped flat-leaved parsley*
- *1½ teaspoons Taratoor bi Sade (page 111) or 1 garlic clove, crushed*
- *12 trimmed loin lamb chops*
- *Salt and freshly ground pepper*

In a small saucepan, slowly melt the *samneh* or butter over low heat. Add all the spices, the mint and the parsley, stir once or twice, then remove from the heat. Stir in the *taratoor* (or crushed garlic) and leave for at least 1 hour at room temperature to allow all of the flavors to mingle.

Season the lamb chops with salt and pepper to taste. Melt the seasoned *samneh*, if it has congealed, and brush the meat with it. Cook the chops over grey-ashed coals or under a preheated broiler for about 6–8 minutes a side, until the outside is well-browned but the inside is still pink. Transfer the chops to serving plates and pour over the remaining seasoned *samneh* or butter. This goes well with *Imjadra* (page 98) or *Batatas bi Houmus* (page 100).

GRAINS AND VEGETABLES
KHUDRAWAT, ROZ WI BURGHUL

ZUCCHINI WITH WALNUTS
KOUSA IN GAMAEL

SERVES 4–6

Although walnuts appear less in Lebanese recipes than pine nuts and pistachios – walnuts are more usually associated with Turkish cuisine – they are still a valued ingredient in many dishes, both desserts and savories.

Heat the butter or oil in a heavy skillet and sauté the zucchini, stirring them, for about 5 minutes, or until soft. Season with salt and pepper, then stir in the walnuts and allspice. Combine well, take off the heat and scatter the parsley on top. Serve immediately.

◆ *5 tablespoons butter or olive oil*
◆ *1½ pounds zucchini, washed, trimmed and thinly sliced*
◆ *Salt and freshly ground black pepper*
◆ *scant 1 cup walnut halves, chopped*
◆ *Large pinch of allspice*
◆ *2 tablespoons finely chopped parsley*

PASTA WITH LEMON AND OIL
MACARONA BI LAEMON

SERVES 4–6

Recipes for a simple type of pasta can be found in old Arab recipe books, although there was never much traditional use of pasta in Lebanon. However, macaroni, tagliatelle and other Italian-style durum-wheat pastas have now become widespread there – treated with typical Middle-Eastern flair.

- ◆ *1 pound macaroni or spaghetti*
- ◆ *1 cup finely chopped parsley*
- ◆ *5 or 6 finely chopped*
- *fresh mint or basil leaves*
- ◆ *scant ½ cup olive oil*
- ◆ *Juice of 1 lemon*
- ◆ *Salt and freshly ground pepper*

Bring a large saucepan of salted water to the boil, then add the pasta and a drop or two of oil. Bring back to the boil and simmer for about 15 minutes, or until just tender. Drain the pasta thoroughly before returning it to the pan.

Add the finely chopped herbs and toss with the pasta. Add the olive oil, lemon juice and salt and pepper to taste, and continue to toss until the pasta has absorbed most of the liquid. The dish may be served either hot or cold.

VEGETABLE LAYER
MOUSAKHA'A

SERVES 6

The name is the same as for the Greek dish of egg plant, ground meat, potatoes and cheese, but the combination of vegetables and spices in this dish is utterly Middle Eastern. This is a main dish casserole, made complete with rice or burghul.

- ◆ *1½ pounds egg plant or zucchini, washed, trimmed and cubed*
- ◆ *Salt and freshly ground pepper*
- ◆ *Olive oil*
- ◆ *2 large onions, sliced*
- ◆ *1 sweet green bell pepper, cored, seeded and chopped*
- ◆ *1 garlic clove, finely chopped*
- ◆ *1½ pounds ripe tomatoes, peeled, seeded and chopped*
- ◆ *½ cup Labneh (page 53)*
- ◆ *2–3 eggs, beaten (optional)*

Put the egg plant cubes in a strainer and sprinkle with salt. Allow them to drain for 30 minutes, then pat dry. (This process draws bitter juices out of the egg plant. If using zucchini, it is not necessary to salt and drain them.)

Pour about 2 tablespoons olive oil into a skillet, and sauté the onions over medium heat for about 5 minutes, or until limp. Stir in the green bell pepper and cook for a further 3–4 minutes, until it is softened and the onions are lightly colored. Stir in the garlic and remove from the heat. Use a slotted spoon to transfer the onions, bell pepper and garlic to a plate.

Heat more oil – about 3–4 tablespoons – and stir in the cubed egg plant or zucchini. Cook, stirring, for about 8 minutes, until they are colored and beginning to soften. Pour off the excess oil and spread the egg plant or zucchini over the bottom of the pan. Place the onions and bell pepper evenly on top. Pour over the chopped tomatoes, and pat them even. Add about 1 cup water to the pan, cover and simmer over low heat for 30 minutes. In the last 10 minutes of cooking time, top with spoonfuls of the *labneh* and the beaten egg, if desired. Cover and simmer until the eggs are set. Season the dish to taste and then serve.

LENTILS AND RICE
MUDARDARA

SERVES 6–8

Biblical anthropologists believe that Esau's "mess of pottage", as recorded in the Book of Genesis, was composed of rice and lentils – a version of the *mudardara* eaten today. Every family has its special way of making this staple, varying the proportions and/or the spicing. Cinnamon is not traditional, but it is sometimes added, since it is believed to increase sexual prowess and give strength to the ill.

- ◆ *1 cup brown lentils, washed and picked over*
- ◆ *5 tablespoons olive oil*
- ◆ *4 large onions, sliced*
- ◆ *1⅓ cups long-grain rice, washed*
- ◆ *Salt and freshly ground pepper*
- ◆ *¼ teaspoon cinnamon (optional)*

Bring a large saucepan of water to the boil, add the lentils, cover and simmer for about 25–30 minutes, until just soft.

Meanwhile, heat the olive oil in a heatproof casserole with a cover, and stir in the sliced onions. Cook over medium-low heat until the onions are limp and just beginning to color. Remove half of them with a slotted spoon and set aside. Cook the remainder, being careful not to let them burn, until brown and glazed. Remove from the heat and transfer the onions to a bowl.

Drain the cooked lentils thoroughly, reserving the cooking liquid. Return the lightly cooked onions to the casserole and stir in the rice. Cook until the rice is just transparent, then stir in the drained lentils, salt and pepper to taste, the cinnamon, if desired, and enough of the cooking liquid to cover well. Cook the "pottage", covered, over low heat until the rice has absorbed all the water. If the rice and lentils are not tender yet, add a little more of the lentil liquid and cook until done. Stir in the caramelized onions and serve immediately.

LENTILS AND BURGHUL
IMJADRA

SERVES 6

This is a Lebanese alternative to *Mudardara* (above) and, like that dish, serves as a staple of the poor. It is seen less in Beirut and the towns than in the countryside, where burghul still reigns supreme. It makes a substantial dish with a poached or fried egg on top of each serving. (Cooked chick-peas can be substituted for the cooked lentils.)

- ◆ *5 tablespoons olive oil*
- ◆ *3 onions, thinly sliced*
- ◆ *1 cup brown lentils, washed and picked over*
- ◆ *1½ cups medium-ground burghul*
- ◆ *Salt and freshly ground pepper*
- ◆ *Cayenne pepper*

Heat the oil in a skillet. Fry the onions until they are limp and lightly colored – about 8–10 minutes. Remove about a third of the onions with a slotted spoon and reserve; continue to cook the remaining onions until they are browned. Reserve them.

In a heatproof casserole, cook the lentils in water to cover for about 25 minutes or until just tender. (Add more water during cooking, if necessary, but do not make it too soupy.) Add the burghul, the light-colored onions, salt, pepper and cayenne to taste. Stir to combine, cover, and let the burghul soak up the remaining moisture (add a bit more, if necessary) for about 10–12 minutes. Stir in the browned onions and serve immediately.

RICE WITH PINE NUTS AND CURRANTS
PILAU RICE

SERVES 4

Pilau rice has infiltrated Lebanon from the east – India and Iran – and from Turkey, to the north. It can contain influences from any of these cultures: pine nuts or pistachios, tamarind juice or saffron, currants or white raisins. This is a fairly simple version, which is often served molded to accompany roasted fowl or other main courses.

- scant ½ cup olive oil
- 2 small onions, finely chopped
- 4 tablespoons pine nuts
- 2 tablespoons currants
- ½ teaspoon saffron threads
- 2¾ cups long-grain rice
- Salt and freshly ground pepper
- Fresh parsley and coriander
- Ground paprika

Heat the olive oil over medium heat and sauté the chopped onions until they are limp – about 6–8 minutes. Add the pine nuts and sauté for a few minutes more, until both the onions and nuts are lightly colored. Stir in the currants, saffron and rice, and cook for about 1 minute or until the rice is just transparent.

Add salt to taste and pour in water to cover, about 2½ cups. Cook, covered, on high heat until the water begins to be absorbed, then turn the heat off and allow it to sit for about 20 minutes, or until all the water is absorbed and the rice tender. If it is still not tender, add a tablespoon or so more water and simmer for a couple of minutes. Then leave to sit for a further 5 minutes.

If desired, press the cooked rice into a mold(s) before turning out onto a plate garnished with parsley and coriander. Dust the rice with paprika.

POTATOES WITH CHICK-PEAS
BATATAS BI HOUMUS

SERVES 6

This is another popular, filling dish, which can also do service as a main course. If served as a vegetarian main course, 1 pound fresh spinach can be stirred into the potatoes and chick-peas in the last 5 minutes of cooking and left to wilt.

- ½ cup olive oil
- 1 large onion, chopped
- 12 ounces small red potatoes, washed and cut into small pieces
- 2 garlic cloves, finely chopped
- 2½ cups cooked and drained chick-peas
- 5 medium tomatoes, peeled, seeded and chopped
- Cayenne pepper
- ½ teaspoon coriander seeds
- Salt and freshly ground pepper
- 1 cup finely chopped fresh parsley

Heat the olive oil in a heatproof casserole with a cover. Add the onion and cook until it is lightly colored and limp. Add the chopped potatoes and the garlic, and cook, stirring, over low heat for 3–4 minutes. Stir in the chick-peas, the tomatoes, cayenne pepper to taste and the coriander seeds.

Cover and simmer for 20 minutes, or until the potatoes are soft. Season to taste and stir in the chopped parsley before serving.

This dish can also be cooled, chilled overnight and served cold.

FRIED POTATOES
BATATA HARRA

SERVES 4–6

These fried potatoes are one of the spiciest dishes from the Lebanese kitchen, where cooks otherwise treat fresh chilies with respect. They are unashamedly oily and garlicky as well, so they are not for the faint-hearted or dyspeptic!

- ◆ *½ cup olive oil*
- ◆ *1½ pounds potatoes, peeled and chopped into small pieces*
- ◆ *Salt and freshly ground pepper*
- ◆ *3 garlic cloves, crushed*
- ◆ *2 hot chilies, seeded and chopped*
- ◆ *1 cup finely chopped coriander*

Heat the olive oil and drop in the potatoes. Fry over medium-hot heat and season to taste. Continue cooking for about 20 minutes until the potatoes are soft. Add the garlic and chilies, and gently toss the potatoes over the heat. Sprinkle over the coriander and serve.

BROWN BEANS WITH HERBS
FUL MEDAMES

SERVES 4–6

These small brown beans are members of the fava family, of a specific type native to Egypt and the Levant. They are served with egg on top for breakfast, mashed into a purée with extra oil and lemon juice for *mezze*, or prepared as in this recipe, for a *mezze*, for a main course with meats, or for a side dish. There are restaurants in the Middle East – Egypt especially – that specialize in *ful* dishes.

- ◆ *1½ cups ful medames (brown beans), washed, picked over and soaked for 24 hours in a cool place*
- ◆ *5 tablespoons olive oil*
- ◆ *Juice of 1 lemon*
- ◆ *3 garlic cloves, crushed*
- ◆ *Salt and freshly ground pepper*
- ◆ *1 teaspoon cumin*
- ◆ *3 tablespoons finely chopped fresh coriander*
- ◆ *Extra olive oil and lemon wedges (optional)*

Drain and rinse the beans. Bring a large saucepan – with just less than twice the volume of water to beans – to the boil and add the beans. Cover, bring to the boil again, reduce the heat and simmer for about 2½ hours, or until the beans are tender. Skim the top of the cooking liquid at the beginning to remove any scum. By the end of cooking, the water should have reduced and thickened. If the beans are still too soupy, strain off some of the liquid.

Stir in the oil, lemon juice, garlic, salt and pepper to taste, cumin and fresh coriander. Transfer the beans to a serving bowl and offer hot, or allow to cool and serve cold, with extra olive oil and lemon wedges.

SWEET POTATO, OKRA AND ONION KEBABS

SERVES 6

This is a modern recipe, combining the traditional vegetables of the countryside – okra and onions – with the more recently introduced sweet potato. The method of cooking, however, is time-honored.

- *24 small okra (ladies' fingers)*
- *3 medium-sized sweet potatoes, peeled and each cut into 8 pieces*
- *24 pickling onions*
- *½ cup olive oil*
- *1 tablespoon honey*
- *Salt and freshly ground pepper*
- *½ teaspoon ground cumin*

Trim off the stem end of the okra, being careful not to cut into the seed chambers.

Bring a large saucepan of water to the boil. Drop in the sweet potato pieces and cook for 5 minutes. Add the onions and cook for 4 minutes, then add the okra and continue to cook for a further 1 minute. Drain the vegetables and plunge them into cold water to stop the cooking. Leave for a few minutes, then drain again. Peel the onions.

Thread the vegetables alternately onto 6 large or 12 small skewers. In a bowl, whisk together the oil, honey, salt and pepper to taste and cumin.

Baste the kebabs with the mixture and place them on a hot to medium-hot barbecue over grey-ashed coals (or alternatively under a preheated broiler). Cook for 8–10 minutes, or until all the vegetables are tender, turning once and basting with the dressing occasionally. Serve immediately.

SAUCES, DRESSINGS AND RELISHES
TARATOOR WI MEKHALEL

PINE NUT SAUCE
TARATOOR BI SONOBA

MAKES ABOUT 1½ CUPS

This is another sauce that is usually partnered with fish, although to Western tastes it marries well with pasta, veal and poultry dishes. Although it is most usually served cold, it can also be used in cooking fish or meat. Try serving veal in the manner of *Vitello Tonnato*, substituting this *taratoor* for the tuna sauce.

- ◆ *1 garlic clove, crushed*
- ◆ *Salt*
- ◆ *2 slices white bread, crusts removed and cubed*
- ◆ *2 cups pine nuts*
- ◆ *¼ teaspoon cayenne pepper*
- ◆ *Juice of 2 lemons*

Mash the garlic as much as possible in a bowl with a pinch of salt. Add the bread cubes, cover with warm water to soak and leave for 10 minutes.

Meanwhile place the pine nuts in the grinder of a blender, or in the bowl of a food processor fitted with a metal blade. When the nuts are finely chopped (if using the grinder, transfer the nuts to a liquidizing bowl), add the soaked bread, squeezed to remove some of the moisture, and the cayenne. Process a short time, then add the lemon juice, a little at a time, with the processor on. The result should be a rich, creamy sauce. If necessary, add a little more water. Serve immediately or cover and chill.

The sauce can be kept refrigerated for about 2 weeks or frozen.

PISTACHIO SAUCE
TARATOOR BI FOSTO

MAKES ABOUT 1 CUP

Like other nut sauces this is cold, but it may be served with hot entrées – over fish or tossed with pasta – or cold, again with fish, veal or chicken. It is very rich, so use it sparingly. In Lebanon and other Arab countries, a very salty, aged cheese called *mesh* would be used, but aged *pecorino* makes an agreeable substitute.

- ◆ *1 cup shelled and toasted pistachios*
- ◆ *1 garlic clove, crushed*
- ◆ *2 tablespoons chopped parsley*
- ◆ *2 tablespoons fresh lemon juice*
- ◆ *3 tablespoons olive oil*
- ◆ *scant ½ cup Greek-style yogurt*
- ◆ *¼ cup grated aged pecorino cheese*

In the bowl of a blender or food processor fitted with a steel blade, put the pistachios, garlic and parsley. Run the processor for a brief time to roughly chop the mixture. Add the lemon juice and process until the mixture becomes smoother. With the processor on, slowly add the olive oil, 1 tablespoon at a time, until the sauce is emulsified. Finally, add the yogurt and cheese, and process until smooth. Transfer the sauce to a bowl and serve immediately or chill.

The sauce may be refrigerated for up to 1 week. It does not freeze well.

COLD ALMOND SAUCE
NOUGADA

MAKES ABOUT 2¼ CUPS

This sweet and garlicky nut sauce is a close relative of *nougat*, a sweet brought home to Italy, Spain and France by the Crusaders. It is commonly served with cold white fish, chicken and turkey.

- ◆ *3 cups ground almonds*
- ◆ *Salt and freshly ground pepper*
- ◆ *¼ teaspoon superfine sugar*
- ◆ *2 garlic cloves, crushed*
- ◆ *Juice of 2 lemons*
- ◆ *½ cup olive oil*
- ◆ *3 tablespoons finely chopped parsley*

In a bowl, combine the ground almonds with salt and pepper to taste and the sugar. Mix well. Mash the garlic into the dry ingredients until it has been ground into the almonds. Slowly stir in the lemon juice and then beat in the olive oil, a little at a time, until the sauce is thick as desired. (This can also be done in a food processor or blender, but the result will lack texture.)

When the sauce is emulsified, stir in the chopped parsley. Serve immediately or cover and chill.

The sauce can be kept refrigerated for 2 weeks, and it can also be frozen.

SESAME SAUCE
TARATOOR BI TAHINI

MAKES ABOUT 1½ CUPS

This is the most frequently encountered of Lebanese sauces. It is served heated or cold with both fish and vegetables. It bears a superficial resemblance to Indonesian peanut sauce *(gado-gado)* in its almost overpowering nuttiness.

◆ *2 garlic cloves, crushed*
◆ *¾ teaspoon salt*
◆ *Large pinch of cayenne*
◆ *1 cup* tahini *paste*
◆ *½ cup lemon juice*

In a bowl, mash the garlic together with the salt and cayenne until it makes a paste. Whisk in the *tahini* with a fork, then thin the mixture with the lemon juice, beating continuously. Serve the sauce immediately or cover and chill.

The sauce can be kept refrigerated for 2 weeks, and it can also be frozen.

CLASSIC VINAIGRETTE

MAKES ABOUT 1 CUP

This can be made into a "classic" vinaigrette, in the French-Lebanese sense, by using the Dijon mustard and the wine vinegar (or a combination of vinegar and juice), or in the Arabic-Lebanese tradition, by omitting the mustard and using only lemon juice.

- ◆ ½ teaspoon Dijon mustard (optional)
- ◆ 3 tablespoons red wine vinegar or lemon juice, or a combination of the two
- ◆ ½ cup olive oil
- ◆ Salt and freshly ground pepper

Combine the mustard, if used, the vinegar/lemon juice and the oil in a bottle with a screw top. Shake hard until the dressing is emulsified. Add salt and pepper to taste and shake again. Use immediately, or keep in a dark, cool place for up to 2 weeks.

MIXED PICKLES
KABBIS

MAKES 1 POUND

Pickles can be mixed together before pickling; as with our Western piccalilli, the best combination is probably cauliflower, small onions, cucumbers and, perhaps, green beans. Otherwise, if you are using vegetables such as small green plum tomatoes or turnips, which do not look appetizing pickled, the pickles are traditionally dyed by adding beetroot juice.

- ◆ 1 pound mixed or selected vegetables: turnips, egg plant, small onions, cauliflower, cucumber, green plum tomatoes, green beans
- ◆ 2 cups white wine vinegar
- ◆ 1 cup water (if desired, use water in which beetroot has been cooked)

Use only very small turnips, egg plant, cucumbers, onions and tomatoes. Blanch the vegetables first, drain thoroughly, then cut them as appropriate.

The turnips, egg plant and cucumbers should be quartered, the tomatoes halved and the onions used whole. The green beans should be cut into 2-inch lengths and the cauliflower cut into florets.

Divide the vegetables between pickling jars or plastic-capped screw-top jars. (Do not use metal-capped jars.) In a pitcher, mix together the vinegar, water (colored or not) and salt. Fill the jars almost to the brim with the vegetables, then pour in the pickling liquid to cover just below the screw top. Tap the jars a couple of times on a hard surface to settle the vegetables and expel the air. Cover each jar with stretched plastic wrap and then with the screw top.

Store the pickles in a cool, dark place for up to 3 months. They are best if left for at least 1 month.

CUMIN-LEMON DRESSING

MAKES ABOUT 1 CUP

This spicy vinaigrette makes an interesting change from the more classic versions. It complements a simple tomato salad, pulses such as cold cooked lentils, or even leftovers – such as cold roast potatoes, cubed and tossed with red onion rings and chopped flat-leaved parsley. That is the way the Lebanese and Syrians use it.

- 1 tablespoon superfine sugar
- ½ teaspoon ground cumin
- Large pinch of turmeric
- 5 tablespoons fresh lemon juice
- ½ cup olive oil

Combine the sugar, cumin, turmeric and lemon juice in a bottle with a screw top. Shake hard to dissolve the sugar, then add the olive oil and shake again until the dressing is emulsified. Use immediately, or store in a cool, dark place for up to 2 weeks.

YOGURT AND CUCUMBER SAUCE

MAKES ABOUT 1 CUP

This is an extremely simple sauce, a relative of the Turkish salad *Caçik* (page 59), which is often served as an accompaniment to *Shwarma* (page 13) or over meat-stuffed vegetables, such as egg plant and zucchini. Mint or coriander, as desired, lends a distinctive flavor.

- 1 garlic clove, crushed
- Salt and freshly ground pepper to taste
- 1 cup Greek-style yogurt
- 1 small or 1½ large
- cucumber, peeled, seeded and grated
- 1 tablespoon finely chopped fresh mint or coriander

In a bowl, mash the garlic and about 1 teaspoon salt together. Stir in the yogurt, cucumber and the mint or coriander. Taste, season further to taste, stir again, and serve immediately or chill.

This sauce can be refrigerated for up to 1 week. It does not freeze well.

PISTACHIO DRESSING

MAKES ABOUT 1 CUP

This is a light salad dressing suited to mixed green salads (see Mixed Bitter Leaf Salad, page 44) or sliced avocados.

- ½ cup olive oil
- 4 tablespoons fresh lemon juice
- 1 teaspoon grated lemon peel
- 4 scallions, finely chopped
- ½ cup crushed salted, shelled pistachios
- Salt and freshly ground pepper

In a bowl, whisk the olive oil into the lemon juice. Add the lemon peel, onion, crushed nuts and season to taste. Whisk again to combine thoroughly, then use immediately or bottle.

The dressing will keep in a cool, dark place for as long as 3 days.

GREEN MAYONNAISE

MAKES ABOUT 2 CUPS

Mayonnaise is not indigenous to Lebanese cuisine; yogurt or *tahini* traditionally does service when a creamy cold sauce/dressing is called for. However, the demands and preferences of a multitude of Western visitors – particularly the French – imposed their influence, and mayonnaise has become commonplace at large hotels and Continental-style restaurants. It often comes from a bottle, however, "improved" with herbs to impart an interesting Middle-Eastern tang.

- ◆ *1½ cups homemade or good commercial mayonnaise*
- ◆ *¾ cup finely chopped coriander*
- ◆ *¾ cup finely chopped flat-leaved parsley flat-leaved parsley*
- ◆ *4 tablespoons finely chopped fresh dill*
- ◆ *Large pinch cayenne*
- ◆ *2 tablespoons fresh lemon juice*

Combine all the ingredients in a blender or food processor fitted with a metal blade. Process until the mayonnaise is smooth and thickly green-flecked.

Use immediately or chill for up to 3 days.

LEMON RELISH

This zesty chutney has its roots in North African cuisine, where whole pickled lemons are frequently used in cooking. It has been adapted to serve as a sophisticated accompaniment to fish or fowl by French-trained Lebanese cooks, who have substituted white wine for the brine more commonly encountered in North African countries.

- ◆ 10 large lemons
- ◆ 2 tablespoons sunflower oil
- ◆ 2 small onions, finely chopped
- ◆ 1 cup dry white wine scant 1 cup superfine
- ◆ sugar
- ◆ ½ teaspoon cayenne pepper
- ◆ ½ teaspoon cumin seeds ½ teaspoon freshly
- ◆ ground black pepper

Using a vegetable peeler, remove the peel from all 10 lemons in large strips, including as little pith as possible. Chop the peel finely and reserve.

Take 2 of the peeled lemons, cut the flesh away from the pith and roughly chop the fruit. Pick out the seeds and discard them.

In a heavy saucepan, heat the oil and add the chopped onion. Sauté carefully for about 10 minutes until it is limp, but not colored. Stir in the peel, chopped lemon flesh, white wine, sugar and spices. Cook over a medium-high heat for about 20 minutes, until the liquid has almost disappeared and the relish is syrupy.

Transfer the relish to a bowl to cool, then chill. Serve immediately or keep chilled and well covered for up to 2 weeks.

GARLIC SAUCE
TARATOOR BI SADE

Although this is called a sauce and is used as such, particularly with poultry and lamb dishes, it is also useful as a garlic-flavored base for a wide variety of other dishes. Thinned with yogurt, it makes a delicious, if powerful, dip. It is glorious when used to replace some of the milk in mashed potatoes, and completely changes classic ratatouille. Use your imagination – and courage!

- ◆ 45 garlic cloves, peeled and crushed
- ◆ ½ cup olive oil
- ◆ Juice of 1 lemon

Traditionally, this is made by hand, pounding the garlic with a mortar and pestle and then beating in the olive oil and lemon juice. Today it is more easily made in a food processor fitted with a metal blade, or in a blender.

Put the garlic into the processor bowl and blend briefly to chop the garlic finely. Then slowly add the oil in a stream with the processor on. You should have a smooth purée. Finally, add the lemon juice. Blend briefly and transfer to a bowl. Serve immediately or cover and chill.

The sauce can be kept refrigerated for 2 weeks or more, or frozen.

SATSUMA DRESSING

MAKES ABOUT 1 CUP

This sweet-tangy dressing goes marvellously well with tart fruit salads (like Grapefruit and Avocado Compote, page 62) or over chicken, turkey – or, in a non-Lebanese mode – ham salad.

- *2 tablespoons honey*
- *1 teaspoon finely grated satsuma peel*
- *½ cup freshly squeezed satsuma juice*
- *2 tablespoons freshly squeezed lemon juice*
- *3 tablespoons sunflower oil*

Place the honey and satsuma peel in a bowl, and carefully beat in the satsuma juice and lemon juice. When fully combined, beat in the oil. Use the dressing immediately or bottle it.

The dressing will keep up to 2 weeks when stored in a cool, dark place.

BREADS AND DESSERTS
KHOUBZ WI HAELAWIYAT

LEBANESE BREAD
KHOUBZ

MAKES 8 ROUNDS

Versions of this bread are found all over the Arab world, made at village bakeries and in backyard ovens of packed earth. The recipe is a simple one, but the bread itself is heavenly – a light, puffy round with a slightly gritty quality. It must be eaten immediately, however, as it becomes hard and crumbly as it stands, unless it is quickly covered.

- ◆ 3 cakes fresh or 2 packets dry yeast
- ◆ 8 cups chapati flour or strong white bread flour
- ◆ ½ teaspoon salt
- ◆ ¼ cup olive oil
- ◆ Chapati flour or cornmeal

In a bowl combine ¼ cup lukewarm water with the fresh yeast. Let it stand for about 3 minutes, then stir to make sure that all of the yeast is dissolved. Allow to rest in a warm place for 6 minutes, or until it has doubled in size.

Put the flour in a large, warmed bowl and stir in the salt. Make a well in the center and pour in the yeast mixture. Add the oil and 2 cups lukewarm water, working the latter in a few tablespoons at a time. Add a little more, if necessary, to make a firm dough that can be picked up and removed to a floured work surface.

Knead the dough, pressing, pushing and folding it, for about 20 minutes, or until it is smooth and elastic. Transfer the dough to the bowl, cover with a cloth and leave in a warm place for 2 hours, until doubled in bulk and bubbly. Place the dough on the work surface and "knock it back" with a couple of knuckle punches. Divide the dough into 8 pieces and shape them into balls.

Scatter the chapati flour or cornmeal on the work surface and roll out 4 of the balls into 8-inch rounds. As you roll out each round, place it on a baking sheet covered with a cloth. Repeat with the remaining 4 balls on another baking sheet. Leave both covered sheets of bread to rise for another half hour. Preheat the oven to 400°.

Place both sheets, one above the other, as low in the oven as possible. Bake at this level for 5 minutes, then move them to the center of the oven, placing the sheet that was lower on top. Continue baking for a further 4–5 minutes, or until the rounds are puffed and golden. Remove from the oven and serve immediately. The rounds can be kept covered in foil in a low oven or warm place, if not needed immediately, but they will loose their puffy quality quickly.

SESAME BREAD RINGS
KA'AK

MAKES 12

In Lebanon these sesame rings are made by bakeries; in some other countries they are more commonly sold on street corners. The *mahlab* (page 15) imparts a typical flavor found only in Arab baked goods. Broken into pieces, *ka'ak* makes a good alternative to pita or *khoubz* for dips.

- ½ cake fresh or 1 packet dry yeast
- 1 teaspoon superfine sugar
- 2 cups strong white bread flour
- ½ teaspoon salt
- 1 teaspoon ground mahlab
- 1 tablespoon semnah or melted butter
- 1 egg, beaten
- 3 tablespoons sesame seeds

In a bowl combine ¼ cup lukewarm water with the yeast and sugar. Let it stand for about 3 minutes, then stir. Allow to rest in a warm place for about 6 minutes.

Put the flour in a large, warmed bowl, and stir in the salt and ground *mahlab*. Make a well in the center and pour in the yeast and sugar mixture. Work the *semnah* or butter into the flour and add 5–6½ tablespoons water to the dough, a spoonful at a time, until you have a firm dough that can be moved to a floured work surface.

Preheat the oven to 300°.

Knead the dough, pressing, pushing and folding, for about 10 minutes, until it is smooth and elastic. Transfer to a bowl, cover with a cloth and leave in a warm place for 15 minutes.

"Knock back" the dough with a couple of punches and divide it into 12 pieces. On a floured work surface, roll each piece into a long "sausage" about the thickness of a finger. Shape the sausage into a circle – or, less authentically but more decoratively, into a criss-crossed pretzel shape.

Place the rings on an oiled baking sheet, cover with a cloth and leave to rise for about 15 minutes. Brush each ring with some beaten egg and sprinkle with sesame seeds. Bake in the oven for about 30–35 minutes, until golden.

Transfer the rings to a cake rack to cool for 10 minutes before serving. The rings freeze successfully.

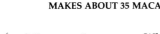

PINE NUT MACAROONS

MAKES ABOUT 35 MACAROONS

These cookies are a contribution of the once-large Italian community in Beirut; they combine the flavors of Rome and the Middle East to great effect.

- 2 cups marzipan
- 1¾ cups superfine sugar
- ¼ teaspoon vanilla or lemon extract
- Pinch of cinnamon
- Pinch of allspice
- 2 egg whites
- 4 tablespoons pine nuts
- Icing sugar

In a large bowl, using an electric mixer, beat together the marzipan and sugar until creamy; beat in the vanilla or lemon extract and the spices. One at at time, beat in the egg whites.

Preheat the oven to 300°.

When the mixture is smooth, drop the batter by small spoonfuls onto baking sheet(s) covered with greaseproof paper, leaving space between each mound, and stick the pine nuts into the macaroons so that they look like porcupine quills.

Bake the macaroons for about 15 minutes, until the cookies and nuts are light gold. Remove the sheets from the oven, lift the edges of the greaseproof paper, and pour a thin stream of water under the paper to loosen the macaroons. Lift them with a spatula to wire racks and let them cool completely before serving.

The macaroons will keep in an airtight container for as long as 1 week.

ARMENIAN FLATBREAD

MAKES 2 ROUND LOAVES

The sizeable Armenian community in Lebanon – established there as a result of several Turkish massacres – have made several contributions to the national cuisine. This flatbread makes an interesting change to *khoubz* when bread is called for. Each loaf will serve about 4–6.

- ◆ 1½ *cakes fresh or 1 packet dry yeast*
- ◆ 1 *teaspoon superfine sugar*
- ◆ 3 *cups strong bread flour*
- ◆ 1 *teaspoon salt*
- ◆ 1 *teaspoon* semnah *or soft butter*
- ◆ 2 *tablespoons yogurt*
- ◆ 2–3 *tablespoons poppy seeds*

In a bowl, combine 2 cups lukewarm water with the yeast. Let it stand for about 3 minutes, then stir in the sugar and allow to stand in a warm place for about 10–12 minutes, or until it is bubbly and doubled in size.

Put half of the flour into a large, warmed bowl and stir in the salt. Make a well in the center and work in the *semnah*, then add the yeast mixture, little by little, until you have a workable dough.

Remove the dough to a floured work surface and knead it, pressing, pushing and folding it, for about 10 minutes, adding as much of the remaining flour as is necessary to make it smooth and elastic. Transfer it back to the bowl, cover with a cloth and leave to rise in a warm place for about 45 minutes, or until it is doubled in size.

Preheat the oven to 400°. Knock back the dough with a couple of knuckle punches, and divide it in half. Shape it into 2 balls, then roll out each ball into a 15-inch-diameter circle. Brush the two loaves with the yogurt, thinned with a little water, and sprinkle over the poppy seeds. Bake for 20–25 minutes until the bread becomes golden brown and puffed.

You can freeze one or both loaves, if desired, to be warmed up at a later date.

YOGURT WITH HONEY AND NUTS

SERVES 4

This dish can be made very simply, using yogurt straight from the carton. However, it benefits from letting the yogurt drain for a little while to thicken it – though not as long as for *labneh*.

- ◆ 2½ *cups Greek-style sheep's yogurt*
- ◆ ½ *cup whole blanched almonds, roughly chopped*
- ◆ ½ *cup whole pistachios,*
- *halved*
- ◆ 2 *tablespoons honey*
- ◆ 1 *teaspoon ground cinnamon*
- ◆ 1 *teaspoon ground nutmeg or cardamom*

Pour the yogurt into a strainer lined with damp muslin or a clean, fine-weave cloth. Let it drain in this position for about 2–3 hours.

Preheat the oven to 350°.

Mix the two nuts on a baking sheet and toast until golden – about 8–10 minutes. Transfer the nuts into a bowl and stir in the honey and cinnamon.

Transfer the drained yogurt into 4 small bowls and spoon over the honeyed nuts. Sprinkle each portion with a little of the nutmeg or cardamom, as preferred. Serve immediately.

SEMOLINA LEMON CAKE
BASBOOSA

MAKES A 8 X 12-INCH CAKE

This lemon-flavored cake is popular from Turkey to Egypt, and is served either as a teatime treat or as a dessert. The traditional version is richer in *semnah* than this one, which cuts the fat content considerably.

- *generous 1 cup superfine sugar*
- *2 cups semolina*
- *½ teaspoon bicarbonate of soda*
- *1½ cups Greek-style yogurt*
- *4 tablespoons semnah or melted butter*

- *18–24 whole blanched almonds*

SYRUP
- *generous 1 cup superfine sugar*
- *4 tablespoons fresh lemon juice*
- *Few drops rosewater*

Make the syrup first. Put 1½ cups water, the sugar and the lemon juice into a heavy-based saucepan and simmer, stirring, until the sugar has dissolved. Then bring the mixture to a vigorous boil, and cook until it has the consistency of syrup or registers 220° on a sugar thermometer. Put aside to cool.

Preheat the oven to 350°.

To make the cake, mix together the first 3 dry ingredients. Beat in the yogurt with a wooden spoon, then beat in the *semnah* or melted butter. Scrape the batter into a well-greased 8 x 12-inch baking pan, and bake for about 15 minutes. Top the cake with the blanched almonds, spacing them 3 or 4 nuts across and 6 down. Continue to bake the cake for a further 30 minutes or until golden.

Cool the cake for about 10 minutes, then cut it into squares or diamonds. Pour the cooled syrup over the cake slowly, allowing it to soak in; use only enough to saturate the cake; it should not be soggy. Serve at room temperature.

The cake will keep in an airtight container for anything up to a week.

STUFFED DATES
TAMAR BI LOHZ

MAKES 12 OF EACH

Stuffed dried fruits – sweetmeats – are part of traditional Arab hospitality, offered to guests to while away the time while talking and/or drinking coffee or tea. The old recipes for some fillings are very sweet – simply pastes of sugar and ground almonds or flower waters. This version, which can be adapted to dried prunes, substituting walnuts for the almonds, is more appealing to modern tastes.

- ◆ *12 plump medjul dates*
- ◆ *½ cup* anari *or ricotta cheese*
- ◆ *1 teaspoon superfine*

- *sugar*
- ◆ *1 teaspoon finely grated fresh lemon peel*
- ◆ *12 whole almonds*

Carefully slit the dates and remove the pits; gently open up the hole created. Set aside.

In a bowl combine thoroughly the cheese, sugar and lemon peel. Divide the mixture between the 12 dates, pushing it into the cavities and molding the dates around the filling. Push an almond into the top of each date. Arrange attractively on a small serving plate.

HONEY CAKES

MAKES ABOUT 40

These cookie-like cakes combine three favorite Middle-Eastern flavors: honey, cinnamon and lemon. The recipe is a variation of a Jewish favorite; in the 1970s the Jewish community was still a small but influential part of Beirut.

- ◆ *2 cups* semnah *or olive oil*
- ◆ *1¼ cups light brown sugar*
- ◆ *1 tablespoon ground cloves*
- ◆ *1 tablespoon ground cinnamon*
- ◆ *1 teaspoon grated lemon peel*
- ◆ *Juice of 2 lemons*
- ◆ *½ cup honey*
- ◆ *½ cup milk*
- ◆ *4½ cups flour*

- ◆ *2 tablespoons baking powder*

GLAZE
- ◆ *2 cups water*
- ◆ *1 cup honey*
- ◆ *generous 1 cup superfine sugar*
- ◆ *1 teaspoon fresh lemon juice*
- ◆ *⅔ cup chopped mixed fruit*

In a bowl, beat together the *semnah* or oil and the sugar with an electric mixer until creamy. Add the cloves, cinnamon, lemon peel and juice, and continue beating for about 5 minutes until thoroughly combined. Beat in the honey and milk. On low speed, add the flour and baking powder a little at a time. Continue to mix slowly for between 10 and 15 minutes until you have a smooth dough.

Preheat the oven to 350°.

Pick out pieces of dough and roll into plum-sized balls. Flatten the balls between the hands and make a slight indentation across the center. Place on greased baking sheets. Bake for about 20 minutes, or until they are lightly golden.

Just before the cakes are done, heat the water and stir in the honey and sugar. Bring the mixture to a boil; stir until the sugar is dissolved. Lower the heat and simmer for about 5 minutes; the syrup should thicken slightly. Take the mixture off the heat and stir in the lemon juice.

When the cakes are done, remove one at a time from the baking sheets with a spatula and dip into the syrup to coat thoroughly. Place the cakes on a rack, sprinkle with the chopped fruit, and let the cakes become sticky-dry. They will keep in an airtight container, but separate the layers with greaseproof paper.

CINNAMON-PISTACHIO CRESCENTS

MAKES ABOUT 48 CRESCENTS

The crescent or half-moon shape has always been a popular one in Arab lore. These sweet pastries bear some resemblance to miniature French croissants, but with a distinctly Levantine flavor.

◆ 1½ cakes fresh or 1
   packet dry yeast
◆ 2 tablespoons superfine
   sugar
◆ 2½ cups flour
◆ 1 cup melted butter
◆ 2 eggs, beaten

FILLING
◆ 1 tablespoon ground
   cinnamon
◆ 1 cup light brown sugar
◆ 1 cup finely crushed
   pistachios

In a bowl, combine ¼ cup lukewarm water with the yeast. Leave it to rest for 3 minutes, then stir in the sugar and leave for about 5 minutes to allow the sugar to dissolve.

Put the flour in a large bowl, make a well and stir in the yeast mixture, the melted butter and the beaten eggs. Mix with the hands until well combined. Form into a ball, cover the bowl with plastic wrap and chill for at least 4 hours or overnight.

Preheat the oven to 350°.

In a bowl, mix together the cinnamon, brown sugar and nuts. Transfer the ball of dough to a floured work surface and divide it into 6 equal balls.

Roll out one ball into an 8-inch round. Spoon out one-sixth of the cinnamon-nut mixture onto a plate. Press the dough round into the mixture, cover with another plate, and turn the circle backwards onto the second plate. Shake any cinnamon mixture remaining on the plate onto the round. Divide the dough circle into 8 wedges and roll each wedge up, beginning at the wide end. Curve the ends in a half-moon shape. Let the crescents rest for 20 minutes before putting them in the oven for baking.

Repeat the process with the remaining dough balls and cinnamon-nut mixture. Bake the crescents in batches on oiled baking sheets for 15 minutes, or until they are golden.

Some or all of the crescents can be frozen to be warmed up at a later time.

PHYLLO AND NUT PASTRIES
BAKLAVA

MAKES A 8 X 12-INCH CAKE

This recipe has variants all over the Middle East. Although we are perhaps more familiar with the Greek or Turkish version, containing walnuts and using honey in the syrup, the Lebanese use pistachios and/or cashews, and substitute orange blossom water for honey. When shaped into small "cigars", they are called *Asabieh*.

- *1 pound commercial phyllo pastry sheets*
- *2 cups semnah or sweet butter, melted*
- *4 tablespoons sunflower oil*
- *3½ cups shelled pistachios or cashews, finely chopped*
- *1 tablespoon superfine sugar*
- *½ teaspoon ground cinnamon*

SYRUP
- *1¾ cup sugar*
- *1 tablespoon fresh lemon juice*
- *1 tablespoon orange blossom water*

Make the syrup. Combine the sugar, lemon juice and ¾ cup water in a heavy saucepan, and simmer over medium heat until the sugar dissolves. Bring the syrup to the boil and cook vigorously for 5 minutes, until it thickens and reaches 220° on a sugar thermometer. Remove the pan from the heat, stir in the orange blossom water, let it cool, then chill it.

Preheat the oven to 350°.

Take the phyllo sheets out of the packet and cover with a damp cloth. Generously grease the bottom and sides of an 8 x 12-inch baking sheet with some of the butter, then mix the remaining butter with the sunflower oil.

Unroll or unfold two sheets of the phyllo, and drape one into the baking sheet, pressing it into the corners. Brush the sheet with some of the *semnah*/butter and oil, and place the other sheet on top. Brush that sheet with the fat as well, then fold down the two pieces of excess phyllo pastry into the baking sheet, and brush with oil and butter. Repeat the process with 2 more sheets of pastry. Continue until half the phyllo sheets have been used.

In a bowl, mix together the chopped nuts, sugar and cinnamon. Scatter the mixture over the phyllo in the baking sheet and pat it down evenly. Cover the nuts with two more sheets of phyllo pastry, brushed with the *semnah*/butter and oil and folded down. Finish with pairs of the remaining sheets of oiled phyllo, and brush the top with the remaining butter and oil mixture.

Score the top into 2-inch diamond-shaped servings. Bake the *baklava* for 45 minutes at 325°, then to 400° for 20 minutes, until the top is crisp and golden brown.

Remove the *baklava* from the oven, pour over as much cooled syrup as the cake can absorb, and let it cool. Serve at room temperature or chilled.

STUFFED DOUGH PASTRIES
MAM'OUL

MAKES ABOUT 30 PASTRIES

These round or egg-shaped little *petits fours* have much the same consistency as Scandinavian or Dutch *spritz* cookies. They can be seen lined up on the counters of Middle Eastern pâtisseries, dusted with bright green crushed pistachio.

- *1½ sticks sweet butter*
- *3 cups flour*
- *1 tablespoon rosewater*
- *2 tablespoons milk*
- *Icing sugar*
- *2 tablespoons finely crushed or ground pistachio nuts*

DATE FILLING
- *1 cup chopped sugared dates*

NUT FILLING
- *1 cup pistachios or walnuts*
- *superfine sugar*

Make the date filling first. Pour ½ cup water over the chopped dates, and stir over low heat until the dates and water have become an almost dry mush. Reserve.

Cut the butter into the flour and mix together with the fingers; add the rosewater and just enough milk to bind the dough. Continue to work until the dough is soft and pliable. Divide the dough into 30 small balls and then into two groups of 15 balls each.

Flatten a ball slightly and press the side of your index finger down the center to form a hollow. Fill carefully with a little of the date mixture, and re-shape the dough to enclose it, making a round or an oval cookie. Repeat this process of filling with the 14 remaining balls in the group.

Flatten and fill the remaining 15 balls in the same way, but using the crushed pistachios or walnuts and a pinch of sugar.

Preheat the oven to 325°.

Place the pastries on a baking sheet and score lengthwise along the top with a small fork. Bake for about 20–25 minutes; they should not be allowed to brown. Remove from the oven and allow them to cool and harden, then roll in the icing sugar. Take a pinch of the finely crushed or ground pistachio nuts, and sprinkle it down the scored tops of the *mam'oul*.

The cookies will keep in an airtight container for about 1 week.

CINNAMON ICE CREAM

MAKES ABOUT 2½ CUPS

Ice cream, unlike sherbet, is not a traditional Arab or Lebanese sweet. However, as elsewhere throughout the modern world, it has become an accepted part of the culture. This cinnamon ice cream is redolent of the spice market. It goes equally well with fresh fruit salad or *Basboosa* (page 117).

- *2 cups heavy cream*
- *2 egg whites*
- *2 teaspoons ground*
- *cinnamon*
- *scant 1 cup sugar*

Place the cream in a large bowl and stir 2 tablespoons cold water into it. Put the cream and the metal whisks from an electric mixer into the refrigerator, and chill for about 1 hour.

Remove the whisks and cream from the refrigerator and whisk the cream until it has trebled in volume. In another bowl, beat the egg whites until they hold stiff peaks. Gently fold the cinnamon and sugar into the cream, then follow with the beaten egg whites.

Pour the mixture into a plastic container and freeze for 4 hours. Remove from the container into the bowl of a food processor fitted with a metal blade, and process until the ice cream is smooth. Return to the container and freeze for at least 6 hours or overnight.

LEBANESE BREAD PUDDING
OSMALIYEH

SERVES 6

This Arabian dessert is variously made with phyllo pastry, bread or sweet cookies, but this version is the most homely – as bread pudding should be.

- ◆ *Oil for frying*
- ◆ *6–7 individual rounds of khoubz (Arab bread) or pita, split and torn into shreds*
- ◆ *¾ cup plump raisins*
- ◆ *1 cup mixed almonds and pistachios pistachios*
- ◆ *½ cup dried chopped ready-to-eat apricots*
- ◆ *generous ½ cup milk*
- ◆ *1 cup heavy cream*
- ◆ *generous ½ cup sugar*
- ◆ *1½ teaspoons ground cinnamon*

Heat the oil until it is very hot and test with a shred of bread. If it turns a golden brown, then add more pieces and fry the bread in batches. Drain on paper towels.

Spread two-thirds of the fried bread across the bottom of a baking pan, overlapping the pieces. Sprinkle the raisins, nuts and apricots over it evenly. Cover with the remaining fried bread, roughly crushed.

Preheat the oven to 400°.

In a saucepan, stir together the milk, the cream and three-quarters of the sugar. Bring to the boil, then remove from the heat and pour over the bread and fruit mixture in the baking pan.

Mix together the remaining sugar and the cinnamon, and sprinkle over the top of the pudding. Bake for 20 minutes, until browned and bubbling. Serve immediately.

PISTACHIO-ORANGE CAKE

This is another Lebanese syrup cake. The invention of a French-trained chef from Beirut, it reveals its European provenance in the use of ground nuts in the batter and liqueur in the syrup.

- 3 large eggs
- 1/3 cup sugar
- 1/2 teaspoon vanilla or lemon extract
- 1 1/2 teaspoons finely grated orange peel
- Pinch of cinnamon
- Pinch of cream of tartar
- 2 cups shelled pistachios, finely ground
- 1/4 cup ground ka'ak or

crisp breadcrumbs

SYRUP
- generous 1/2 cup superfine sugar
- 2 tablespoons fresh orange juice
- 2–3 kumquats, thinly sliced
- 2 tablespoons Cointreau or Grand Marnier

Make the syrup first. In a heavy-based saucepan, combine the sugar, orange juice and sliced kumquats, and 1/2 cup water. Simmer over moderate heat until the sugar is dissolved, then bring to the boil and cook until the syrup has thickened (and registers 220° on a sugar thermometer). Take off the heat and stir in the orange liqueur. Leave to cool.

Preheat the oven to 350°.

To make the cake, separate the 3 eggs and beat the egg yolks with the sugar and vanilla in a bowl with an electric mixer until the mixture is light yellow. Stir in the grated peel and cinnamon. In another bowl, beat the egg whites with the cream of tartar until they hold soft peaks. In a third bowl, mix together the ground nuts and ka'ak crumbs. Fold one-third of the whites into the egg yolk mixture, then fold in the remaining whites, alternating with the ground nuts mixture. Combine everything gently but thoroughly.

Pour the batter into a well-greased 9-inch square cake pan, and bake for about 25 minutes or until the top is golden. Remove from the oven, and let the cake cool for about 10 minutes, then divide into squares and diamonds and pour over the cooled kumquat syrup. Serve the cake at room temperature.

The cake will keep for 2 days in an airtight container.

ORANGE SORBET
SHARBAT BI BORTUAN

Everyday Arab *sharbat* is a very sweet flavored syrup to be diluted and sipped rather than eaten. It is sold on street corners and served in homes. Adding egg white to lighten flavored crushed ice was a refinement of the sultans to the sherbet – an invention of the Mogul emperors.

- 8 juicy oranges
- generous 1 cup superfine sugar
- 2–3 tablespoons fresh

lemon juice
- 1 1/2 teaspoons orange flower water
- 1 large egg white
- Fresh mint

Thinly peel 2 of the oranges, trying to get as little pith as possible. In a food processor fitted with a metal blade, process the peel and sugar until the mixture is as well combined and mushy as possible. Transfer it into a saucepan and add 1/2 cup water. Stir over high heat and bring the mixture to the boil, then lower the heat, cover and simmer for about 5 minutes. Cool, then chill until very cold.

Squeeze the oranges and measure out 3 1/2 cups of juice into a large bowl. Stir in the syrup, 2 tablespoons lemon juice, 1 teaspoon orange flower water, and the egg white. Stir to combine, but do not beat.

Transfer the mixture to a freezer container and freeze for 5 hours or so, or until slushy. Scoop out the sherbet into the food processor, taste, and add extra lemon juice or orange flower water to taste. Blend until the ice crystals are broken down. Return to the container and freeze overnight. Serve in bowls garnished with sprigs of fresh mint.

YOGURT AND ORANGE MOUSSE CAKE

SERVES 6

This is another "modern" dessert, with the flavors and spirit of the old Levant married to the health concerns of the new. It is also very simple to make.

- ◆ 3 large eggs, separated
- ◆ ½ cup milk
- ◆ 1 cup Greek-style yogurt
- ◆ ½ teaspoon grated orange peel
- ◆ 4 tablespoons fresh orange juice
- ◆ generous 1 cup sugar
- ◆ 2 tablespoons flour
- ◆ 1 teaspoon vanilla extract
- ◆ Sweetened fruit yogurt (optional)

Preheat the oven to 350°.

In a bowl with an electric mixer, beat the separated egg yolks until thickened and pale. Add the milk and yogurt, grated peel and orange juice, then beat in ¾ of the sugar, flour and vanilla until the mixture is smooth.

In a large bowl beat the egg whites on medium speed until they are foamy. Turn the speed up to high, and beat in the remaining sugar until stiff peaks form.

Gently fold the yolk mixture into the whites until all is combined. Pour the batter into a 9-inch square cake pan.

Place the pan in a larger container and pour in boiling water until it comes halfway up the outer sides of the cake pan. Bake the cake in the oven for about 30 minutes or until it is golden. Serve with sweetened fruit yogurt, if desired.

INDEX